Market Microstructure

A Deep Dive into Financial Market Behavior & Market Mechanisms

Daniel Ashford

© 2024 by Daniel Ashford

All rights reserved.

No part of this publication may be reproduced, distributed, or transmitted in any form or by any means, including photocopying, recording, or other electronic or mechanical methods, without the prior written permission of the publisher, except in the case of brief quotations embodied in critical reviews and certain other noncommercial uses permitted by U.S. copyright law.

This book is intended to provide general information on the subjects covered and is presented with the understanding that the author and publisher are not providing legal, financial, or professional advice or services. While every effort has been made to ensure the accuracy and completeness of the information contained herein, neither the author nor the publisher guarantees such accuracy or completeness, nor shall they be responsible for any errors or omissions or for the results obtained from the use of such information. The contents of this book are provided "as is" and without warranties of any kind, either express or implied.

Readers are advised to consult a qualified professional for guidance on specific legal or financial issues. The information and strategies discussed in this book may not be suitable for every individual and are not guaranteed or warranted to produce any particular results. Neither the author nor the publisher shall be liable for any loss, damage, or other issues that may result from the use of or reliance on the information provided in this book.

No representation is made that the quality of the information provided is greater than that which can be obtained from professional services. In no event will the author or publisher be liable for any direct, indirect, incidental, consequential, or other damages arising out of the use of the information in this book.

The content of this book is not intended as legal or financial advice, nor should it be used as a basis for any decision or action that may affect your business or personal finances. Readers should consult their own legal or financial advisors for such advice. Any reliance on the material in this book is at the reader's own risk.

PREFACE

Have you ever wondered how stock prices are determined or what happens when you place a buy or sell order? Financial markets are fascinating, and at its core lies market microstructure. This field explores the mechanisms that govern the behavior of financial markets, shedding light on the interplay between buyers, sellers, intermediaries, and the rules that shape the trading process.

In this book, we'll look at what drive the prices of stocks, bonds, currencies, and other financial instruments. We'll explore the numerous factors that influence market dynamics, from the role of supply and demand to the impact of information flow and trader psychology.

One of the key aspects we'll look into is the structure of financial markets themselves. You'll learn about the different types of market structures, including exchanges, over-the-counter (OTC) markets, and the increasingly prevalent alternative trading systems. We'll examine how these structures facilitate the efficient matching of buyers and sellers, and the mechanisms that ensure fair and orderly trading.

Throughout the book, you'll gain insights into the critical role played by market intermediaries, such as market makers and high-frequency traders. These participants have a vital role in providing liquidity and ensuring the smooth functioning of markets. We'll explore the strategies they employ, the risks they face, and the regulatory frameworks that govern their activities.

We'll also explore trading strategies, from traditional arbitrage techniques to cutting-edge algorithmic and high-frequency trading approaches. You'll learn how traders and investors leverage these strategies to capitalize on market inefficiencies and exploit fleeting opportunities.

Importantly, we'll look into the behavioral aspects of trading, examining the psychological biases and emotional factors that can influence decision-making in the markets. Understanding these dynamics is vital for developing a well-rounded perspective on market microstructure and making informed investment decisions.

Technology has been a driving force in the evolution of financial markets, and we'll dedicate a chapter to exploring the impact of technological advancements on market microstructure. From the rise of high-frequency trading to the advent of cryptocurrencies and decentralized finance, we'll explore how technology is reshaping the trading landscape.

Finally, we'll look ahead to the future trends and emerging developments that are set to shape the market microstructure landscape in the years to come. From the potential impact of artificial intelligence and machine learning to evolving regulation, we'll provide a glimpse into what the future may hold for this dynamic field.

Whether you're a finance professional, a student, or simply someone with a keen interest in understanding the inner workings of financial markets, this book will serve as a clear and accessible guide to market microstructure. We'll break down complex concepts into accessible language, ensuring that readers from diverse backgrounds can grasp this fascinating subject.

TOPICAL OUTLINE

Chapter 1: Introduction to Market Microstructure

- Definition and Importance
- Historical Evolution of Market Microstructure
- Overview of Financial Markets
- Key Concepts in Market Microstructure
- Role of Market Intermediaries
- Market Microstructure Theories
- Impact of Technology on Market Microstructure
- Market Microstructure Research
- Market Microstructure in Different Asset Classes
- Future Directions in Market Microstructure

Chapter 2: Market Mechanisms and Structures

- Order Types and Trading Processes
- Market Participants and Their Roles
- Order Matching and Execution
- Different Types of Market Structures (exchanges, OTC markets, etc.)
- Designing Efficient Markets
- Dark Pools and Alternative Trading Systems
- Clearing and Settlement Processes
- Market Fragmentation and Interconnectedness

Chapter 3: Price Formation and Discovery

- The Role of Supply and Demand
- Price Discovery Mechanisms
- Impact of Information on Prices

Chapter 4: Market Liquidity

- Definition and Measurement of Liquidity
- Factors Affecting Liquidity
- Liquidity and Market Efficiency
- Liquidity Risk Management
- Liquidity Provision Incentives and Obligations

Chapter 5: Order Flow and Order Book Dynamics

- Understanding Order Flow

- Structure of the Order Book
- Order Book Imbalances and Price Movements

Chapter 6: Market Efficiency and Inefficiency

- The Efficient Market Hypothesis
- Causes of Market Inefficiency
- Implications for Traders and Investors
- Market Anomalies and Patterns
- Limits to Arbitrage

Chapter 7: The Role of Market Makers

- Functions and Responsibilities
- How Market Makers Influence Liquidity
- Risks and Challenges Faced by Market Makers
- Market Making Obligations and Privileges
- Inventory Risk Management by Market Makers

Chapter 8: Trading Strategies

- Market Making Strategies
- Arbitrage and Statistical Arbitrage
- Algorithmic and High-Frequency Trading
- News-Based and Event-Driven Strategies
- Execution Strategies and Algorithms

Chapter 9: Behavioral Aspects of Trading

- Psychology of Traders and Investors
- Behavioral Biases in Trading
- Impact of Sentiment on Market Microstructure

Chapter 10: High-Frequency Trading and Technology

- Evolution of High-Frequency Trading
- Impact of Technology on Trading
- Technological Challenges and Advancements
- Co-location and Proximity Hosting Services
- Latency Arbitrage Strategies

Chapter 11: Regulation and Market Microstructure

- Key Regulatory Bodies and Their Roles

- Major Regulatory Frameworks
- Impact of Regulation on Market Behavior
- Regulatory Challenges and Responses

Chapter 12: Market Crises and Microstructure

- Historical Market Crises and Their Causes
- Role of Market Microstructure in Crises
- Lessons Learned and Preventive Measures

Chapter 13: Quantitative Methods in Market Microstructure

- Statistical Tools and Models
- Predictive Analytics and Market Trends
- Applications of Machine Learning
- Agent-Based Modeling and Simulation
- Natural Language Processing for News Analytics

Chapter 14: Future Trends in Market Microstructure

- Emerging Technologies and Their Impact
- Evolution of Trading Practices
- Future Regulatory and Market Structure Changes

Appendix

Afterword

TABLE OF CONTENTS

Chapter 1: Introduction to Market Microstructure ... 1
Chapter 2: Market Mechanisms and Structures ... 21
Chapter 3: Price Formation and Discovery ... 34
Chapter 4: Market Liquidity ... 38
Chapter 5: Order Flow and Order Book Dynamics ... 46
Chapter 6: Market Efficiency and Inefficiency ... 52
Chapter 7: The Role of Market Makers ... 60
Chapter 8: Trading Strategies ... 67
Chapter 9: Behavioral Aspects of Trading ... 76
Chapter 10: High-Frequency Trading and Technology ... 81
Chapter 11: Regulation and Market Microstructure ... 88
Chapter 12: Market Crises and Microstructure ... 96
Chapter 13: Quantitative Methods in Market Microstructure ... 102
Chapter 14: Future Trends in Market Microstructure ... 112
Appendix ... 118
Afterword ... 128

CHAPTER 1: INTRODUCTION TO MARKET MICROSTRUCTURE

Definition and Importance

At its core, market microstructure is the study of how financial markets work at the most fundamental level. It zooms in on the specific rules, processes, and behaviors that shape the trading of stocks, bonds, currencies, and other assets. Think of it like a microscope for markets. Instead of looking at the big picture (like overall stock market trends), we examine the tiny details:

- **The Players:** Who's buying and selling? We analyze the different types of traders: high-frequency firms, institutional investors, individual retail traders, etc.
- **The Venue:** Where does trading happen? Exchanges, dark pools, over-the-counter markets – each has its own unique characteristics.
- **The Rules:** How does trading work? We examine the specific order types (limit, market, etc.), the matching algorithms that bring buyers and sellers together, and the fee structures.

Why Should You Care?

Now, you might be wondering, "Why should I care about these nitty-gritty details?" Well, market microstructure is incredibly important for several reasons:

1. **Price Formation:** The microstructure directly affects how prices are determined. Understanding these mechanisms can help you anticipate price movements and make better-informed trading decisions.
2. **Liquidity:** One of the key goals of any market is to provide liquidity, which means the ability to buy or sell assets quickly and easily. The microstructure has a massive impact on how liquid a market is.
3. **Transaction Costs:** The costs associated with trading (commissions, bid-ask spreads, etc.) are directly influenced by the microstructure. Knowing how these costs arise can help you minimize them.
4. **Fairness and Efficiency:** We want markets to be fair and efficient. By studying the microstructure, we can identify potential problems (like high-frequency trading front-running) and design solutions to improve market quality.
5. **Regulation:** Regulators use insights from market microstructure to create rules and policies that promote fair and orderly markets. Understanding this field can help you navigate the regulatory landscape.

Beyond Trading

The importance of market microstructure extends beyond just trading. It's a fascinating field with connections to other areas, like:

- **Behavioral Economics:** How do traders' behaviors and biases affect market outcomes?
- **Game Theory:** How do different trading strategies interact and compete?
- **Information Economics:** How does information flow through markets and impact prices?

The Future of Market Microstructure

The field of market microstructure is constantly evolving. New technologies (like blockchain) and regulatory changes are reshaping how markets function. Staying ahead of the curve requires a deep understanding of these underlying mechanisms.

Historical Evolution of Market Microstructure

The historical evolution of market microstructure is a fascinating journey reflecting the changing dynamics of financial markets. Let's take a walk through time:

Early Days: The Open Outcry

Picture a bustling trading floor with traders shouting, waving their arms, and signaling to each other. This was the open outcry system, the dominant method for centuries. It was loud, chaotic, but it worked. Prices were determined through face-to-face negotiation, and trust and relationships had a big role.

The Rise of Technology: Electronic Trading

The late 20th century saw a technological revolution that transformed markets. Electronic trading platforms emerged, replacing the open outcry system. Now, traders could submit orders through computers, and sophisticated algorithms matched buyers and sellers. This increased trading speed and efficiency but also introduced new challenges.

Fragmentation and Dark Pools

As electronic trading grew, so did market fragmentation. Instead of a single central exchange, trading activity became spread across multiple venues. Dark pools, private trading platforms where orders aren't publicly displayed, also gained popularity.

This increased competition among trading venues and led to concerns about transparency and fairness.

High-Frequency Trading (HFT)

The early 2000s marked the rise of high-frequency trading (HFT). These firms use powerful computers and algorithms to execute trades in fractions of a second. While HFT increased liquidity and narrowed spreads, it also raised concerns about market manipulation and instability.

Regulatory Response

As market structures evolved, regulators struggled to keep up. The 2008 financial crisis highlighted the need for stronger oversight. New regulations, like the Dodd-Frank Act in the U.S. and MiFID II in Europe, aimed to increase transparency, curb excessive risk-taking, and protect investors.

The Rise of Alternative Trading Systems (ATS)

In recent years, we've seen the growth of alternative trading systems (ATS), also known as multilateral trading facilities (MTF). These are trading venues that operate alongside traditional exchanges, often with different rules and fee structures. This has further increased competition and given traders more choices.

The Impact of Blockchain

The emergence of blockchain technology and cryptocurrencies has the potential to disrupt traditional market structures. Decentralized exchanges (DEXs) are challenging the dominance of centralized exchanges, and tokenization of assets could change how we trade everything from stocks to real estate.

Key Trends and Challenges

Looking ahead, several key trends and challenges will shape the future of market microstructure:

- **Data and Analytics:** The ability to collect and analyze massive amounts of market data will become even more critical for understanding and predicting market behavior.
- **Artificial Intelligence:** AI and machine learning will play a growing role in developing trading strategies, risk management, and market surveillance.
- **Sustainability:** Investors are increasingly demanding transparency and accountability on environmental, social, and governance (ESG) issues, which could reshape market practices.

Overview of Financial Markets

Let's break down the key types of financial markets, which are the arenas where market microstructure comes into play:

1. Equity Markets (Stock Markets)

- **What's traded:** Shares of companies, representing ownership stakes.
- **Why it matters:** Stock markets are where companies raise capital to grow their businesses, and where investors seek returns on their investments.
- **Microstructure focus:** Order types (market, limit, etc.), trading algorithms used by exchanges, and the impact of high-frequency trading.

2. Fixed Income Markets (Bond Markets)

- **What's traded:** Debt instruments like government bonds, corporate bonds, and municipal bonds.
- **Why it matters:** Bond markets provide funding for governments and corporations, and offer investors relatively stable income.
- **Microstructure focus:** Dealer markets, price discovery mechanisms, and the role of institutional investors.

3. Foreign Exchange Markets (Forex)

- **What's traded:** Currencies from different countries.
- **Why it matters:** The largest and most liquid market globally, facilitating international trade and investment.
- **Microstructure focus:** Decentralized nature, role of banks and electronic communication networks (ECNs), and impact of algorithmic trading.

4. Commodity Markets

- **What's traded:** Raw materials like oil, gold, agricultural products, etc.
- **Why it matters:** These markets influence the prices of essential goods and serve as a hedge against inflation.
- **Microstructure focus:** Futures contracts, delivery mechanisms, and the impact of weather and geopolitical events.

5. Derivatives Markets

- **What's traded:** Financial contracts whose value is derived from an underlying asset (e.g., options, futures, swaps).

- **Why it matters:** Used for hedging risk, speculation, and gaining exposure to various assets.
- **Microstructure focus:** Clearinghouses, margin requirements, and the potential for systemic risk.

Other Key Market Types:

- **Money Markets:** Short-term debt instruments (e.g., Treasury bills, commercial paper).
- **Real Estate Markets:** Properties (residential, commercial, industrial).
- **Insurance Markets:** Policies that transfer risk from individuals to insurance companies.

Understanding Market Structure

Each market type has a unique structure that influences how trading occurs.

- **Centralized vs. Decentralized:** Some markets have a single exchange, while others operate across a network of dealers or electronic platforms.
- **Order-Driven vs. Quote-Driven:** In order-driven markets, prices are determined by matching buy and sell orders, while in quote-driven markets, dealers set prices.
- **Transparent vs. Opaque:** Some markets have publicly visible order books, while others (like dark pools) operate with less transparency.

Key Concepts in Market Microstructure

Understanding the key concepts is fundamental to grasping the intricacies of market microstructure.

1. **Order Book Dynamics:** The order book is the heart of many markets. It's a record of all the buy and sell orders waiting to be executed. Understanding how orders are placed, modified, and cancelled provides insights into supply and demand dynamics, price discovery, and potential market movements.

2. **Bid-Ask Spread:** This is the difference between the highest price a buyer is willing to pay (bid) and the lowest price a seller is willing to accept (ask). The spread is a key indicator of market liquidity and trading costs. A narrow spread suggests a liquid market with tight competition, while a wide spread indicates a less liquid market with higher trading costs.

3. **Market Orders vs. Limit Orders:** Market orders are executed immediately at the best available price, prioritizing speed. Limit orders

specify a maximum buying price or minimum selling price, giving traders more control but potentially delaying execution.

4. **Liquidity Providers (Market Makers):** These are individuals or firms that continuously quote both bid and ask prices, providing liquidity to the market. They profit from the bid-ask spread and are necessary in ensuring smooth and efficient trading.

5. **Price Discovery:** This is the process of determining the "fair" price of an asset through the interaction of buyers and sellers. It's influenced by factors like supply and demand, information flow, and trading behavior.

6. **Transaction Costs:** These are the costs associated with trading, including explicit costs like commissions and fees, as well as implicit costs like the bid-ask spread and market impact (the effect of a large order on price).

7. **Information Asymmetry:** This refers to situations where some market participants have more information than others. This can lead to adverse selection (informed traders taking advantage of uninformed traders) and impact market efficiency.

8. **Market Impact:** This is the price change caused by a trade. Large orders can move prices significantly, creating challenges for institutional investors and traders who need to execute large positions.

9. **Volatility:** This measures the degree of price fluctuations in a market. High volatility can create opportunities for traders but also increases risk.

10. **Market Efficiency:** This refers to how quickly and accurately prices reflect all available information. Efficient markets are difficult to beat, as prices adjust rapidly to new information.

11. **High-Frequency Trading (HFT):** HFT firms use powerful computers and algorithms to execute trades at incredibly high speeds. They contribute to liquidity but have also raised concerns about market manipulation and unfair advantages.

12. **Regulatory Landscape:** Market microstructure is heavily influenced by regulations designed to ensure fair and orderly markets. These regulations cover areas like market manipulation, insider trading, and trade reporting.

13. **Technological Advancements:** New technologies like blockchain and artificial intelligence are reshaping market microstructure, creating new opportunities and challenges for traders and investors.

Role of Market Intermediaries

Market intermediaries are entities that facilitate transactions between buyers and sellers. They don't own the assets being traded, but they play a vital role in bringing parties together and ensuring smooth, efficient trading. Some common types of intermediaries include:

- **Brokers:** They act as agents for buyers and sellers, executing trades on their behalf in exchange for a commission.
- **Dealers:** They buy and sell assets from their own inventory, making a profit on the bid-ask spread.
- **Exchanges:** They provide a centralized platform where buyers and sellers can meet and trade.
- **Clearinghouses:** They act as intermediaries between buyers and sellers, guaranteeing the completion of trades and managing risk.
- **Custodians:** They hold assets on behalf of investors, providing safekeeping and other services.

The Essential Functions of Intermediaries

Intermediaries perform several crucial functions that contribute to the overall health and efficiency of financial markets:

1. **Providing Liquidity:** Intermediaries like dealers and market makers ensure that there are always buyers and sellers available, allowing investors to trade quickly and easily. This is essential for price discovery and preventing large price swings.
2. **Reducing Search Costs:** Imagine trying to find someone who wants to buy the exact number of shares you want to sell at the precise price you want. Intermediaries eliminate this hassle by bringing buyers and sellers together in a centralized marketplace.
3. **Facilitating Price Discovery:** By aggregating information from many different buyers and sellers, intermediaries help determine the fair market price of an asset. This is crucial for ensuring that prices reflect all available information.
4. **Mitigating Counterparty Risk:** Clearinghouses act as central counterparties (CCPs) in many markets, guaranteeing that trades will be completed even if one party defaults. This significantly reduces the risk of trading.
5. **Enhancing Transparency:** Exchanges and other trading platforms provide information about prices, trading volume, and other market data. This transparency helps investors make informed decisions and promotes fair and orderly markets.
6. **Providing Other Services:** Intermediaries offer a variety of other services, such as research, analysis, and execution services, that can benefit investors and traders.

The Evolving Role of Intermediaries

The role of market intermediaries is constantly evolving as new technologies and regulations emerge. For example:

- **Electronic Trading:** The rise of electronic trading platforms has automated many of the functions traditionally performed by human traders, increasing speed and efficiency.
- **High-Frequency Trading (HFT):** HFT firms have become major players in many markets, providing liquidity and tightening spreads, but also raising concerns about market fairness and stability.
- **Regulatory Changes:** New regulations, such as MiFID II in Europe, have introduced stricter rules for market intermediaries, aiming to increase transparency and protect investors.

Market Microstructure Theories

These theories aim to explain the observed patterns and behaviors in financial markets, especially at the micro-level of individual trades and order flows.

1. Inventory Models

- **Core Idea:** Dealers and market makers act like inventory managers. They adjust prices to balance their holdings and manage risk.
- **Key Insight:** The bid-ask spread reflects the dealer's inventory risk and the costs associated with holding inventory. Wider spreads signal higher risk or cost.

2. Information-Based Models

- **Core Idea:** Trading is driven by differences in information among market participants. Informed traders try to profit from their superior knowledge, while uninformed traders try to learn from market prices.
- **Key Insight:** Price changes reflect the arrival of new information and the subsequent trading activity as investors update their beliefs.

3. Strategic Trading Models

- **Core Idea:** Traders are strategic agents who anticipate the actions of others and try to maximize their profits. They consider factors like order size, timing, and the presence of other traders.
- **Key Insight:** Large traders, like institutional investors, can strategically break up their orders to minimize market impact and transaction costs.

4. Order Flow Models

- **Core Idea:** Order flow, the stream of buy and sell orders, is a key determinant of price dynamics. Aggregated order flow can reveal market sentiment and predict short-term price movements.
- **Key Insight:** Analyzing order flow can help traders identify trends and potential reversals, as well as understand the motivations of other market participants.

5. Adverse Selection Models

- **Core Idea:** Informed traders have an informational advantage and can selectively trade against uninformed traders. This can lead to adverse selection, where uninformed traders end up on the losing side of trades.
- **Key Insight:** Market makers widen spreads to protect themselves from adverse selection, and traders may try to signal their information (or lack thereof) through their trading behavior.

6. Market Making Models

- **Core Idea:** Market makers are useful in providing liquidity and facilitating trading. They face a trade-off between earning the bid-ask spread and the risk of holding inventory.
- **Key Insight:** Market makers adjust their quotes based on their inventory position, order flow, and market conditions. Understanding their behavior is essential for traders who interact with them.

Let's look at some specific models:

Kyle Model (1985): The Dance of Informed and Uninformed Traders

Think of this model like a poker game. Informed traders (those with secret knowledge) try to profit without revealing their hand. Uninformed traders watch the informed players' bets (trades) to figure out what they know. The market maker (the casino) sits in the middle, trying to set fair odds (prices) without getting tricked.

Key takeaway: The more informed traders there are (higher lambda), the riskier it is for the market maker, leading to wider bid-ask spreads.

Glosten-Milgrom Model (1985): Market Makers and Adverse Selection

This model focuses on the market maker's perspective. Imagine they're playing a guessing game, trying to figure out which traders are informed. They set bid and ask prices to protect themselves from being taken advantage of by informed traders.

Key takeaway: The bid-ask spread compensates market makers for the risk of trading with informed traders.

Garman Model (1976): The Market Maker's Inventory Balancing Act

This model treats the market maker like a shopkeeper managing inventory. They want to keep the right amount of stock on hand to meet demand, but not too much that it ties up capital or risks going bad. They adjust prices to encourage buying or selling depending on their inventory level.

Key takeaway: The market maker's inventory and risk preferences affect the bid-ask spread and price movements.

Madhavan-Smidt Model (1991): The Impact of Strategic Traders

This model throws strategic traders into the mix. These traders carefully plan their trades, considering factors like market impact and transaction costs. They try to outsmart both the market maker and other traders.

Key takeaway: Strategic traders' actions can impact the bid-ask spread and pricing strategies of market makers.

Easley-O'Hara Model (1987): Information, the Price Mover

In this model, information is king. The arrival of new information (like a company earnings report) triggers a flurry of trading as investors update their beliefs. This model helps us understand how information affects prices and trading behavior.

Key takeaway: The probability of information events and the level of informed trading influence the bid-ask spread and trading volume.

Admati-Pfleiderer Model (1988): Timing is Everything

This model is all about the timing of trades. Informed traders strategically choose when to trade to maximize profits and minimize their impact on the market.

Key takeaway: The timing of trades can reveal information and affect price formation, sometimes leading to concentrated trading and increased liquidity at certain times.

Stoll Model (1978): The Bid-Ask Spread Breakdown

This model is like a recipe for the bid-ask spread. Stoll breaks it down into three main ingredients:

- **Order processing costs:** The cost of executing trades (think technology, personnel, etc.).
- **Inventory holding costs:** The cost of holding assets in inventory (think risk and capital tied up).
- **Adverse selection costs:** The cost of potentially trading with someone who has better information than you.

Key takeaway: The bid-ask spread isn't just a random number. It's a reflection of the costs and risks faced by market makers.

Roll Model (1984): Covariance and the Hidden Spread

Roll's model is a bit like a detective story. It looks at the pattern of price changes (covariance) and uses it to uncover the hidden bid-ask spread. The idea is that the spread creates a kind of friction in prices, causing them to bounce around a bit more than they would otherwise.

Key takeaway: Even if you don't see the bid-ask spread directly, its effects are still visible in price patterns.

Microstructure Noise Models: Filtering Out the Noise

Think of these models as noise-cancelling headphones for the market. They help us separate the true signal (changes in fundamental value) from the noise caused by the microstructure itself (things like bid-ask bounces and fleeting imbalances).

Key takeaway: Not every price movement is meaningful. Some of it is just noise created by the mechanics of trading.

Agent-Based Models: The Market as a Complex System

These models are like a computer simulation of a market. We create virtual traders with different strategies and preferences and let them loose to see how they interact. This can help us understand how complex market dynamics emerge from the behavior of individual traders.

Key takeaway: Markets are complex systems where the actions of individual traders can have ripple effects on the whole system.

Amihud-Mendelson Model (1986): The Cost of Illiquidity

This model highlights the importance of liquidity. It argues that illiquid assets (those that are hard to buy or sell quickly) should have higher expected returns to compensate investors for the difficulty of trading them.

Key takeaway: Liquidity isn't just a convenience. It's a valuable feature that affects asset prices.

O'Hara, Parlour, Back-Baruch Models: Market Structure Matters

These models explore how the design of the market itself (e.g., transparency, competition between trading venues) affects liquidity, price discovery, and the behavior of traders and market makers.

Key takeaway: The rules of the game matter. Different market structures create different incentives and outcomes.

Vayanos-Wang, Almgren-Chriss, Obizhaeva-Wang Models: Trading Strategies and Market Impact

These models focus on the strategies traders use to execute large orders and minimize their impact on the market. They also consider how the market responds to these large trades, including the risk of adverse price movements.

Key takeaway: Trading isn't just about buying and selling. It's a strategic game with complex dynamics and potential pitfalls.

Theoretical HFT Models, Limit Order Book Models, Market Fragmentation Models: The Cutting Edge

These models are at the forefront of market microstructure research. They explore the impact of high-frequency trading, the dynamics of limit order books, and the effects of market fragmentation on liquidity, price discovery, and overall market quality.

Key takeaway: Market microstructure is a dynamic and evolving field. New technologies and trading practices are constantly challenging our understanding of how markets work.

Why are Market Microstructure Theories Important?

- **Understanding Price Formation:** They help us understand how prices are determined in different market conditions and how information gets incorporated into prices.

- **Developing Trading Strategies:** They provide insights into optimal trading strategies, such as order placement, timing, and size.
- **Assessing Market Quality:** They help us evaluate the efficiency and fairness of markets, identify potential problems, and design solutions.
- **Guiding Regulatory Policies:** They inform regulators about potential market abuses and help design policies to promote fair and orderly markets.

Impact of Technology on Market Microstructure

It's been a game-changer, reshaping how we trade, who trades, and where trading happens.

1. Electronic Trading: The Rise of the Machines

The shift from open outcry trading floors to electronic platforms was monumental. Computers took over the matching of buyers and sellers, making trading faster, cheaper, and more accessible to a wider range of participants. This also led to the rise of algorithmic trading, where computers execute trades based on pre-programmed instructions.

2. High-Frequency Trading (HFT): The Speed Demons

HFT firms armed with powerful computers and ultra-low latency connections burst onto the scene, executing trades in microseconds. They brought increased liquidity and tighter spreads to markets, but also raised concerns about market fairness, stability, and the potential for an "arms race" in technology.

3. Fragmentation: The Many Faces of Markets

With electronic trading, markets became fragmented. Trading activity spread across multiple exchanges, alternative trading systems (ATS), and dark pools. This increased competition among venues, but also made it more challenging to track prices and understand overall market dynamics.

4. Big Data and Analytics: The Information Advantage

The explosion of market data created new opportunities for analysis and decision-making. Sophisticated algorithms now sift through massive datasets to identify patterns, predict trends, and execute trades. This gave rise to quantitative trading strategies and the importance of data as a competitive advantage.

5. Blockchain and Distributed Ledger Technology (DLT): The Decentralization Movement

Blockchain technology has the potential to disrupt traditional market structures. Decentralized exchanges (DEXs) challenge the centralized model of traditional exchanges, promising increased transparency and security. Tokenization of assets could change how we trade everything from stocks to real estate.

6. Artificial Intelligence (AI) and Machine Learning (ML): The Smart Traders

AI and ML are increasingly being used to develop trading strategies, manage risk, and even predict market movements. These technologies have the potential to transform the role of human traders and create a new breed of "smart" market participants.

The Impact on Market Microstructure

These technological advancements have had a profound impact on market microstructure:

- **Increased Liquidity:** Electronic trading and HFT have made it easier and faster to trade, increasing overall market liquidity.
- **Reduced Transaction Costs:** Competition among trading venues and the automation of trading processes have driven down transaction costs.
- **Increased Volatility:** The speed and interconnectedness of markets, fueled by technology, have led to increased volatility and the potential for flash crashes.
- **New Market Participants:** Technology has lowered barriers to entry, allowing new players like retail traders and fintech firms to participate in markets.
- **Regulatory Challenges:** The rapid pace of technological change has created challenges for regulators who struggle to keep up with new trading practices and technologies.

Market Microstructure Research

This field is constantly evolving, with researchers delving into a wide range of topics to better understand the intricate workings of financial markets.

Key Areas of Research:

1. **Price Formation and Discovery:**
   - Researchers investigate how prices are formed through the interaction of buyers and sellers, and how quickly and accurately those prices reflect new information.

- They study the impact of different order types (market, limit, etc.), trading algorithms, and market structures on price discovery.
- This research helps us understand how efficient markets are at incorporating information and how we can improve price formation mechanisms.

2. **Liquidity and Trading Costs:**
- Researchers analyze the determinants of market liquidity, the ease with which assets can be bought or sold without significantly impacting prices.
- They examine the factors that influence trading costs, such as bid-ask spreads, commissions, and market impact.
- This research is crucial for understanding how to create more liquid and efficient markets, reducing costs for investors and promoting overall market stability.

3. **Market Design and Regulation:**
- Researchers explore how different market designs (e.g., continuous trading, call auctions) and regulatory policies affect market outcomes.
- They study the impact of regulations on market quality, investor protection, and systemic risk.
- This research helps policymakers design rules that promote fair, efficient, and stable markets.

4. **High-Frequency Trading (HFT) and Algorithmic Trading:**
- Researchers investigate the impact of HFT and algorithmic trading on market liquidity, price discovery, and volatility.
- They study the potential risks and benefits of these trading practices and explore how to mitigate any negative consequences.
- This research is critical for understanding the evolving landscape of modern markets and ensuring that technology is used to enhance, rather than harm, market quality.

5. **Market Microstructure and Asset Pricing:**
- Researchers explore the relationship between market microstructure features and asset prices.
- They study how factors like liquidity, trading costs, and information asymmetry affect asset returns.
- This research helps investors understand the risk and return characteristics of different assets and make better-informed investment decisions.

6. **Behavioral Finance and Market Microstructure:**

- Researchers examine how psychological biases and behavioral patterns of traders and investors impact market outcomes.
- They study phenomena like herding behavior, overconfidence, and anchoring bias and how they can lead to market inefficiencies.

- This research helps us understand the role of human behavior in financial markets and develop strategies to mitigate the negative effects of biases.

7. Empirical Studies and Data Analysis:

- Researchers collect and analyze vast amounts of market data to test theories, identify patterns, and uncover new insights.
- They use statistical and econometric techniques to measure market quality, liquidity, and trading costs.
- This research provides empirical evidence to support or challenge existing theories and inform the development of new models.

The Future of Market Microstructure Research:

The field of market microstructure research is constantly evolving, driven by new technologies, regulatory changes, and the growing complexity of financial markets. Some of the exciting areas for future research include:

- The impact of blockchain technology and decentralized finance (DeFi) on market structure.
- The use of artificial intelligence and machine learning to analyze market data and develop trading strategies.
- The implications of climate change and ESG (Environmental, Social, and Governance) factors on market microstructure.

Market Microstructure in Different Asset Classes

Each market has its own unique characteristics, which influence how trading works and the strategies traders use.

Equities (Stocks):

- **Venue:** Primarily traded on stock exchanges (like the NYSE or NASDAQ).
- **Participants:** A mix of institutional investors, retail traders, and high-frequency trading firms.
- **Order Types:** Wide variety of order types, including market, limit, stop-loss, and more complex algorithmic orders.
- **Transparency:** High degree of pre-trade transparency with public order books.
- **Liquidity:** Generally high liquidity, especially for large-cap stocks.
- **Microstructure Concerns:** Impact of HFT on price volatility and fairness, dark pool trading, and potential conflicts of interest between brokers and their clients.

Fixed Income (Bonds):

- **Venue:** Mostly traded over-the-counter (OTC) through dealers.
- **Participants:** Primarily institutional investors like banks, insurance companies, and pension funds.
- **Order Types:** Less standardized than equities, with a focus on negotiated deals and block trades.
- **Transparency:** Lower pre-trade transparency compared to equities.
- **Liquidity:** Can vary significantly depending on the bond issue and market conditions.
- **Microstructure Concerns:** Opaque pricing, potential for dealer markups, and lack of centralized clearing for some bond types.

Foreign Exchange (Forex):

- **Venue:** Decentralized, global market with no central exchange.
- **Participants:** Banks, financial institutions, corporations, and individual traders.
- **Order Types:** Primarily market orders and limit orders, with increasing use of algorithmic trading.
- **Transparency:** Varies depending on the platform and counterparties involved.
- **Liquidity:** Extremely high liquidity, especially for major currency pairs.
- **Microstructure Concerns:** Potential for manipulation, fragmented liquidity across different platforms, and the role of central banks in market intervention.

Commodities:

- **Venue:** Exchanges (like the CME) or OTC.
- **Participants:** Producers, consumers, speculators, and hedgers.
- **Order Types:** Futures contracts are common, with delivery mechanisms playing a key role.
- **Transparency:** Varies depending on the commodity and trading venue.
- **Liquidity:** Can be high for some commodities (like oil and gold) but lower for others.
- **Microstructure Concerns:** Impact of weather events and geopolitical tensions on prices, potential for market manipulation, and delivery squeezes.

Cryptocurrencies:

- **Venue:** Cryptocurrency exchanges (centralized and decentralized).
- **Participants:** A mix of retail investors, institutional investors, and algorithmic traders.

- **Order Types:** Similar to equities, with market and limit orders being common.
- **Transparency:** Varies across exchanges, with some offering public order books and others operating more opaquely.
- **Liquidity:** Highly variable, with some cryptocurrencies having significant liquidity while others are illiquid.
- **Microstructure Concerns:** Wash trading, market manipulation, security risks, and the impact of regulatory uncertainty.

Key Takeaways:

- Market microstructure is not one-size-fits-all. It varies significantly across asset classes due to differences in trading venues, participants, order types, transparency, liquidity, and specific risks.
- Understanding the unique microstructure of each asset class is crucial for developing effective trading strategies and managing risk.
- Market microstructure is constantly evolving, with new technologies and regulatory changes reshaping the landscape.

Future Directions in Market Microstructure

The landscape is constantly shifting, with technological advancements and regulatory changes driving innovation and reshaping how markets function.

1. Decentralized Finance (DeFi) and Blockchain:

- **The Rise of Decentralized Exchanges (DEXs):** These peer-to-peer trading platforms eliminate the need for intermediaries, promising greater transparency and security. Research will focus on how DEXs impact liquidity, price discovery, and market stability.
- **Tokenization of Assets:** Real-world assets like real estate, art, and commodities are being tokenized on the blockchain, opening up new markets and trading opportunities. We can expect research to look into the microstructure of these emerging tokenized markets.

2. Artificial Intelligence (AI) and Machine Learning (ML):

- **Enhanced Trading Strategies:** AI and ML will play an increasingly important role in developing sophisticated trading algorithms that can analyze vast amounts of data, identify patterns, and execute trades with greater precision. Research will explore the impact of AI on market efficiency and the potential risks of overreliance on algorithms.
- **Market Surveillance and Risk Management:** Regulators and market participants will leverage AI and ML to detect market manipulation, insider

trading, and other fraudulent activities. Research will focus on developing robust AI-powered surveillance systems and risk management tools.

3. The Evolution of High-Frequency Trading (HFT):

- **The Arms Race Continues:** As technology advances, the race for speed and low latency will intensify. Research will explore the limits of HFT and the potential for new technologies like quantum computing to disrupt the field.
- **Regulatory Scrutiny:** Concerns about the impact of HFT on market fairness and stability will lead to ongoing regulatory scrutiny and potential changes in market rules. Research will analyze the effectiveness of different regulatory approaches and their impact on market quality.

4. Big Data and Alternative Data:

- **Uncovering Hidden Signals:** The explosion of data from social media, news feeds, satellite imagery, and other sources offers new opportunities for market analysis. Research will focus on how to extract meaningful signals from this alternative data and incorporate it into trading strategies.
- **Data Privacy and Security:** As the use of data becomes more prevalent, concerns about privacy and security will become increasingly important. Research will explore ways to balance the benefits of data-driven insights with the need to protect sensitive information.

5. Sustainability and ESG (Environmental, Social, and Governance) Factors:

- **Impact Investing:** Investors are increasingly demanding transparency and accountability on ESG issues. Research will investigate how ESG factors influence market microstructure, pricing, and investor behavior.
- **Sustainable Finance Regulations:** Regulators are developing new rules to promote sustainable finance and combat greenwashing. Research will analyze the impact of these regulations on market practices and outcomes.

6. The Future of Market Makers and Liquidity Provision:

- **Competition from New Players:** Traditional market makers face competition from new players like HFT firms and algorithmic liquidity providers. Research will explore the changing landscape of liquidity provision and the potential risks and benefits of different models.
- **The Role of Central Bank Digital Currencies (CBDCs):** The introduction of CBDCs could revolutionize payment systems and potentially impact market liquidity. Research will examine the potential consequences of CBDCs for market microstructure.

I hope this glimpse into the future of market microstructure has sparked your curiosity. As we venture further into the 21st century, this field promises to be a hotbed of innovation, with new technologies, regulatory changes, and evolving market dynamics constantly reshaping the landscape.

CHAPTER 2: MARKET MECHANISMS AND STRUCTURES

Order Types and Trading Processes

Think of these as the tools of the trade, each designed for specific scenarios and goals.

Core Order Types

1. **Market Order:**
    - **What it does:** Buys or sells at the best available price *immediately*.
    - **When to use it:** When speed is your priority, and you're okay with potentially getting a slightly worse price if the market is moving.
    - **Example:** "Buy 100 shares of AAPL right now, no matter the price."
2. **Limit Order:**
    - **What it does:** Sets a maximum price you'll pay (buy limit) or a minimum price you'll accept (sell limit).
    - **When to use it:** When you want to ensure you get a specific price or better, but your order might not get filled if the market doesn't reach your limit.
    - **Example:** "Buy 100 shares of AAPL, but only if the price is $150 or lower."

Advanced Order Types

These are variations on the basic market and limit orders, adding more conditions for execution:

3. **Stop-Loss Order:**
    - **What it does:** Triggers a market order to sell if the price falls below a certain level (stop-loss) or buy if it rises above a certain level (stop-buy).
    - **When to use it:** To limit potential losses on a trade or to enter a trade when a certain price level is reached.
    - **Example:** "If AAPL drops to $145, sell my 100 shares immediately."
4. **Stop-Limit Order:**
    - **What it does:** Similar to a stop-loss order, but instead of triggering a market order, it triggers a limit order.
    - **When to use it:** When you want to limit losses *and* ensure you get a certain price or better on the exit, but with the risk of your order not being filled if the market moves quickly.

    - ◦ **Example:** "If AAPL drops to $145, sell my 100 shares, but only if I can get at least $144 per share."
5. **Trailing Stop Order:**
    - ◦ **What it does:** Dynamically adjusts the stop price as the market moves in your favor, locking in profits while letting the trade run as long as it's profitable.
    - ◦ **When to use it:** When you want to capture potential gains but also protect against reversals.
    - ◦ **Example:** "Buy AAPL, and set a trailing stop-loss 10% below the highest price reached."

How Trading Works (Simplified)

1. **You Place an Order:** You tell your broker what to buy/sell, how much, and what type of order to use.
2. **Order Routing:** Your order is sent to the appropriate trading venue (exchange, ATS, dark pool, etc.).
3. **Order Matching:** The trading venue's matching engine tries to match your order with a compatible order from another trader.
4. **Execution:** If a match is found, the trade is executed, and you become the proud owner (or seller) of the asset.
5. **Clearing and Settlement:** Behind the scenes, clearinghouses ensure that both parties fulfill their obligations (delivering cash or assets), and the trade is settled.

Key Takeaways:

- Choosing the right order type is crucial for managing risk and achieving your trading goals.
- Understanding the trading process helps you appreciate the speed and complexity of modern markets.
- Market microstructure constantly evolves, with new order types and trading venues emerging. Staying informed is key to successful trading!

Market Participants and Their Roles

Financial markets are like bustling ecosystems, teeming with a diverse cast of characters, each playing a specific role. Understanding these market participants and their motivations is key to unlocking the secrets of market microstructure. Let's meet some of the main players:

1. Informed Traders:

- **Who they are:** These traders possess valuable information about an asset's future value that isn't yet public knowledge. They could be company insiders, analysts with deep industry knowledge, or simply skilled at interpreting market data.
- **Their role:** They drive price discovery by trading based on their superior information, pushing prices closer to their true value. Their actions are carefully watched by other traders seeking to glean insights.

2. Uninformed Traders:

- **Who they are:** These traders lack access to the same level of information as informed traders. They may be individual investors, less experienced traders, or those relying on public information.
- **Their role:** They provide liquidity to the market by taking the other side of trades initiated by informed traders. Their participation is essential for ensuring that markets function smoothly.

3. Market Makers (Liquidity Providers):

- **Who they are:** These are typically large financial institutions or specialized firms that continuously quote both bid and ask prices for an asset.
- **Their role:** They are the backbone of many markets, providing liquidity by ensuring that there's always someone willing to buy or sell. They profit from the bid-ask spread and help maintain orderly markets.

4. Institutional Investors:

- **Who they are:** These are large organizations like pension funds, mutual funds, insurance companies, and endowments that manage vast amounts of capital.
- **Their role:** They are major players in many markets, with their trades often having a significant impact on prices. They seek to maximize returns for their clients and often employ sophisticated trading strategies.

5. High-Frequency Traders (HFT):

- **Who they are:** These firms use powerful computers and algorithms to execute trades at lightning-fast speeds, often measured in microseconds.
- **Their role:** They provide liquidity and can contribute to price efficiency by quickly incorporating new information into prices. However, their aggressive trading tactics have also raised concerns about market stability and fairness.

6. Retail Traders:

- **Who they are:** These are individual investors who trade for their own accounts, often through online brokerage platforms.
- **Their role:** While their individual trades may be small, their collective actions can have a significant impact on markets, especially in times of high volatility or during social media-driven "meme stock" frenzies.

7. Brokers:

- **Who they are:** They act as intermediaries between buyers and sellers, executing trades on behalf of their clients.
- **Their role:** They provide access to markets, offer trading tools and research, and may advise clients on investment strategies. They earn commissions on trades and are important in facilitating market participation.

8. Exchanges:

- **Who they are:** These are organized marketplaces where buyers and sellers meet to trade securities.
- **Their role:** They provide a centralized platform for trading, establish rules and regulations to ensure fair and orderly markets, and often act as clearinghouses to guarantee the settlement of trades.

Understanding the roles and motivations of these different market participants is essential for analyzing market microstructure. Their interactions create a dynamic and complex ecosystem where prices are formed, liquidity is provided, and information is disseminated.

Order Matching and Execution

Order matching and execution is where the rubber meets the road in market microstructure – where your buy or sell order meets its counterpart and a transaction occurs.

The Order Book: The Central Hub

Many modern markets, especially for stocks and some derivatives, use an order book system. Think of it like a giant bulletin board where buyers and sellers post their intentions.

- **Buy Orders (Bids):** Listed in descending order of price (highest bid at the top). These represent the maximum price buyers are willing to pay.

- **Sell Orders (Asks):** Listed in ascending order of price (lowest ask at the top). These represent the minimum price sellers are willing to accept.

The Matching Engine: The Matchmaker

This is the heart of the trading system. It's a powerful algorithm that continuously scans the order book, looking for matches. A match occurs when a buy order's price is equal to or higher than a sell order's price.

Order Matching Rules: Price-Time Priority

- **Price Priority:** Orders with better prices get priority. Higher bids or lower asks are filled first.
- **Time Priority:** If multiple orders have the same price, the earliest order submitted gets priority.

Types of Order Matching

1. **Continuous Trading:**
    - **How it works:** Matching happens continuously throughout the trading day as orders arrive.
    - **Pros:** Provides immediate liquidity, allowing traders to execute quickly.
    - **Cons:** Can be prone to volatility, especially during periods of high activity.
2. **Call Auctions:**
    - **How it works:** Orders are collected over a period, and then all matched at a single price at a specific time.
    - **Pros:** Can lead to more stable prices and less volatility.
    - **Cons:** Less frequent trading opportunities, may not be suitable for all assets.

Execution: Making the Trade Happen

Once a match is found, the trade is executed. The price at which the trade occurs is the execution price.

- **Market Orders:** Executed instantly at the best available price in the order book.
- **Limit Orders:** Executed only if the market price reaches the specified limit or better. If not, the order remains in the order book until it's either filled or cancelled.

Factors Affecting Execution:

- **Liquidity:** Higher liquidity means more orders in the book, leading to faster and more reliable execution.
- **Volatility:** High volatility can cause rapid price changes, impacting the execution price, especially for market orders.
- **Order Size:** Large orders may have trouble finding enough matching orders at a single price, leading to partial fills or worse prices.

Beyond the Order Book: Other Matching Mechanisms

Not all markets use an order book.

- **Over-the-Counter (OTC) Markets:** Trades are negotiated directly between buyers and sellers, often through dealers.
- **Dark Pools:** These are private trading platforms where orders are not displayed publicly. Matches are made based on specific algorithms and criteria.

Key Takeaways:

- Order matching and execution are the core processes that enable trading.
- The order book and matching engine play a central role in many markets.
- Understanding the different order types and matching mechanisms is crucial for developing effective trading strategies.
- Market microstructure is dynamic, with new technologies and trading venues constantly emerging.

Different Types of Market Structures (exchanges, OTC markets, etc.)

Each one has its own unique way of facilitating trades, impacting things like transparency, liquidity, and price discovery.

1. Exchanges: The Traditional Powerhouses

- **What they are:** Centralized marketplaces with standardized rules and procedures. Think of major stock exchanges like the New York Stock Exchange (NYSE) or the NASDAQ.
- **How they work:** Buyers and sellers submit orders through brokers, which are then matched by the exchange's electronic system.
- **Pros:** High transparency (public order book), strong regulation, and generally good liquidity for listed securities.
- **Cons:** Can be more expensive due to fees, less flexible for large or complex trades.

2. Over-the-Counter (OTC) Markets: The Negotiators' Haven

- **What they are:** Decentralized networks of dealers who trade directly with each other, rather than through a central exchange. Common in bond markets, foreign exchange, and some derivatives.
- **How they work:** Trades are negotiated bilaterally, with prices agreed upon between the buyer and seller.
- **Pros:** Greater flexibility for customizing trades, can be more efficient for large or illiquid securities.
- **Cons:** Less transparency, higher counterparty risk, and potential for price manipulation.

3. Alternative Trading Systems (ATS): The New Kids on the Block

- **What they are:** Electronic trading platforms that operate alongside traditional exchanges. They can be multilateral (matching multiple buyers and sellers) or bilateral (facilitating trades between two parties).
- **How they work:** Similar to exchanges, but often with different rules and fee structures.
- **Pros:** Can offer lower costs, faster execution, and innovative trading features.
- **Cons:** May have less liquidity than exchanges, and regulatory oversight can vary.

4. Dark Pools: The Secret Clubs

- **What they are:** Private trading venues where orders are hidden from the public. They are typically used by institutional investors to execute large trades without revealing their intentions to the broader market.
- **How they work:** Matching is done based on specific algorithms and criteria set by the dark pool operator.
- **Pros:** Can reduce market impact for large trades, offer potential price improvement.
- **Cons:** Lack of transparency raises concerns about fairness and potential for conflicts of interest.

5. Broker-Dealer Internalization: The In-House Matchmaker

- **What it is:** When a brokerage firm matches its clients' buy and sell orders internally, rather than sending them to an exchange or other venue.
- **How it works:** The brokerage firm acts as both the buyer and seller for its clients.
- **Pros:** Can be faster and cheaper for clients, as it eliminates exchange fees.
- **Cons:** Potential for conflicts of interest, as the brokerage firm may not always get the best price for its clients.

6. Cryptocurrency Exchanges: The Wild West

- **What they are:** Online platforms for trading cryptocurrencies like Bitcoin and Ethereum.
- **How they work:** Similar to traditional exchanges, but with unique features like 24/7 trading and different regulatory environments.
- **Pros:** Access to a growing asset class, potential for high returns (and high risks).
- **Cons:** Volatility, security risks, and lack of consistent regulation.

Designing Efficient Markets

Think of it like building a well-oiled machine – every component needs to work together seamlessly to achieve the desired outcome: a market that serves both investors and the broader economy.

Key Goals of Efficient Markets:

1. **Price Efficiency:** Prices should quickly and accurately reflect all available information. This means no one can consistently profit from predictable patterns or outdated news.
2. **Liquidity:** Investors should be able to easily buy or sell assets without causing large price swings. This allows for smooth trading and efficient allocation of capital.
3. **Transparency:** Market participants should have access to reliable and timely information about prices, trading activity, and other relevant data. This fosters trust and promotes fair competition.
4. **Low Transaction Costs:** The costs associated with trading (e.g., commissions, bid-ask spreads) should be minimized. This encourages participation and allows investors to keep more of their returns.

Strategies for Designing Efficient Markets:

- **Market Structure:** Choose the right type of market structure (exchange, OTC, etc.) based on the asset class and desired outcomes. Exchanges offer transparency and liquidity, while OTC markets provide flexibility.
- **Trading Mechanisms:** Design matching algorithms that prioritize fairness, speed, and price improvement. Consider using both continuous trading and auctions to cater to different trading styles.
- **Technology:** Embrace technology to enhance trading efficiency and reduce costs. Implement electronic trading platforms, consider blockchain for increased transparency and security, and explore the potential of AI to optimize order execution.

- **Regulation:** Implement clear and consistent rules to prevent market manipulation, insider trading, and other fraudulent activities. Ensure that regulations promote competition and protect investors without stifling innovation.
- **Market Maker Incentives:** Attract and incentivize market makers to provide liquidity. This can involve offering rebates for providing quotes or reducing regulatory burdens.
- **Information Dissemination:** Ensure that market data is readily available to all participants. This includes pre-trade information (like order book data) and post-trade information (like trade prices and volumes).
- **Investor Education:** Educate investors about market mechanisms, trading strategies, and the risks involved. This helps them make informed decisions and avoid costly mistakes.

The Challenge of Balancing Competing Objectives:

Designing efficient markets isn't easy. There are often trade-offs between different goals. For example, increasing transparency may reduce the willingness of large investors to participate, impacting liquidity. Finding the right balance requires careful consideration and ongoing evaluation.

The Ever-Evolving Landscape:

Market microstructure is a dynamic field. New technologies and trading practices are constantly emerging, requiring ongoing adaptation and innovation. By understanding the principles of efficient market design, we can create markets that better serve investors and the broader economy.

Dark Pools and Alternative Trading Systems

Let's shed some light on the shadowy world of dark pools and alternative trading systems (ATS), two types of trading venues that play a significant role in market microstructure.

Dark Pools: Trading in the Shadows

- **What they are:** Private trading platforms where buy and sell orders aren't publicly displayed. Think of them as exclusive clubs for institutional investors.
- **Their purpose:** To allow large trades to occur without revealing the trader's hand to the broader market. This helps avoid market impact, where large orders can move prices against the trader.
- **How they work:** Orders are matched using various methods, including price-time priority, pro-rata matching, or more complex algorithms.

- **Pros:** Reduced market impact, potential for price improvement compared to public exchanges.
- **Cons:** Lack of transparency raises concerns about fairness, potential for information leakage, and limited access for retail investors.

Alternative Trading Systems (ATS): The New Kids on the Block

- **What they are:** Electronic trading platforms that operate outside of traditional exchanges. They can be multilateral (matching multiple buyers and sellers) or bilateral (facilitating trades between two parties).
- **Their purpose:** To provide alternative venues for trading, often with different rules, fee structures, and technology than traditional exchanges.
- **How they work:** Similar to exchanges, but with more flexibility and innovation. Some ATSs function as dark pools, while others offer transparent order books.
- **Pros:** Increased competition among trading venues, potentially lower costs and faster execution for traders.
- **Cons:** May have less liquidity than exchanges, and regulatory oversight can vary.

The Rise of Dark Pools and ATS:

- **Technological Advancements:** The advent of electronic trading and algorithmic execution has fueled the growth of these alternative venues.
- **Regulatory Changes:** Regulations like Reg NMS in the U.S. have encouraged competition among trading venues, leading to the proliferation of ATSs.
- **Demand for Large-Block Trading:** Institutional investors seeking to minimize market impact have found dark pools and certain ATSs attractive.

Controversies and Concerns:

- **Transparency:** The opacity of dark pools raises concerns about unfair advantages for certain participants and potential market manipulation.
- **Order Routing:** Critics argue that some brokers may not always route orders to the venue with the best price for their clients, potentially leading to conflicts of interest.
- **Market Fragmentation:** The proliferation of trading venues has led to increased fragmentation, making it harder to track prices and understand overall market dynamics.

Clearing and Settlement Processes

Think of this as the behind-the-scenes work that ensures a trade isn't just an agreement, but a completed transaction where everyone gets what they're supposed to.

Clearing: The Record Keeper

- **What it is:** The process of confirming and reconciling trade details between the buyer and seller. Imagine it as a meticulous accountant double-checking every line item in a contract.
- **Why it's important:** Clearing ensures that both parties agree on the terms of the trade (asset, quantity, price) and reduces the risk of errors or disputes.
- **Who does it:** Typically done by a clearinghouse, a central counterparty (CCP) that acts as a middleman between buyers and sellers.
- **How it works:** The clearinghouse compares trade records from both sides, matches them up, and then notifies both parties that the trade is cleared.

Settlement: The Exchange

- **What it is:** The actual exchange of the asset for cash. This is where ownership of the asset officially changes hands.
- **Why it's important:** Settlement finalizes the trade, ensuring that the buyer receives the asset and the seller receives the cash.
- **Who does it:** Usually handled by depositories and custodians, who hold assets on behalf of investors.
- **How it works:** Involves transferring ownership of the asset from the seller's account to the buyer's account, and the corresponding cash transfer in the opposite direction.

T+1 Settlement: The Time Delay

- **What it is:** Most stock trades in the U.S. follow a T+1 settlement cycle (implemented after T+2 was common until 2024), meaning the trade settles one business day after the execution date.
- **Why it's important:** This delay allows time for clearing, verifying ownership, and arranging the transfer of assets and cash.
- **Why it's changing:** There's a push towards shortening the settlement cycle to even same-day settlement to reduce risk and improve market efficiency.

Risks and Challenges in Clearing and Settlement

- **Counterparty Risk:** The risk that one party to the trade won't fulfill their obligations. Clearinghouses help mitigate this risk by guaranteeing the settlement of trades.

- **Operational Risk:** The risk of errors or failures in the clearing and settlement process, which can lead to delays or losses.
- **Cybersecurity Risk:** The risk of cyber attacks that could disrupt the clearing and settlement process or compromise sensitive data.

Market Fragmentation and Interconnectedness

Market fragmentation and interconnectedness are two sides of the same coin in modern market microstructure. They represent both a challenge and an opportunity in today's trading landscape.

Market Fragmentation: The Splintering of Liquidity

- **What it is:** The scattering of trading activity across multiple venues. Instead of one central marketplace, we now have a mosaic of exchanges, alternative trading systems (ATS), and dark pools.
- **The drivers:** Technological advancements (electronic trading), regulatory changes (Reg NMS), and the rise of new trading venues.
- **The impact:**
  - **Pros:** Increased competition among venues can lead to lower fees and innovation in trading technology.
  - **Cons:** Can make it harder to find the best price, as liquidity is spread out. It can also create complexity for traders who need to track multiple markets.

Interconnectedness: The Network Effect

- **What it is:** The linking of different trading venues through electronic networks. This allows orders to be routed and executed across multiple platforms.
- **The drivers:** The need for brokers to find the best prices for their clients and the desire of trading venues to attract order flow.
- **The impact:**
  - **Pros:** Can improve price discovery by aggregating information from different venues. It can also enhance liquidity by allowing access to a wider pool of orders.
  - **Cons:** Can create challenges for market surveillance and regulation, as it becomes more difficult to track trading activity across multiple venues. It can also lead to increased complexity and potential for technological glitches.

The Balancing Act:

Market fragmentation and interconnectedness are interconnected. Fragmentation creates the need for interconnectedness to access liquidity and find the best prices. However, too much fragmentation can lead to inefficiencies and regulatory challenges.

The Future:

The trend towards fragmentation and interconnectedness is likely to continue. New technologies like blockchain could further decentralize markets, while regulatory efforts may aim to address the challenges of fragmentation.

Key Takeaways:

- Market fragmentation is a reality of modern markets, driven by technology and regulation.
- Interconnectedness is essential for accessing liquidity and ensuring efficient price discovery.
- Finding the right balance between fragmentation and interconnectedness is crucial for creating well-functioning markets.

CHAPTER 3: PRICE FORMATION AND DISCOVERY

The Role of Supply and Demand

These are the twin engines that drive prices in every market, from stocks to sneakers.

Supply: How Much is Out There?

- **What it is:** The total quantity of an asset that sellers are willing and able to offer at various prices.
- **How it works:** When the price of an asset rises, sellers are generally more eager to offer their holdings, increasing supply. Conversely, when prices fall, supply tends to decrease as sellers hold back.

Demand: How Much Do People Want?

- **What it is:** The total quantity of an asset that buyers are willing and able to purchase at various prices.
- **How it works:** When the price of an asset falls, buyers are more inclined to purchase, increasing demand. When prices rise, demand typically decreases as buyers become less interested.

The Dance of Supply and Demand:

- **Equilibrium Price:** This is the magical point where supply and demand intersect. At this price, the quantity buyers want to buy matches the quantity sellers want to sell, creating a balanced market.
- **Price Discovery:** This is the dynamic process of finding the equilibrium price. It happens as buyers and sellers constantly interact, adjusting their orders based on the prevailing market conditions.

How Supply and Demand Affect Prices:

- **Excess Demand:** When demand exceeds supply, buyers compete to purchase the limited available assets, driving prices up.
- **Excess Supply:** When supply exceeds demand, sellers compete to attract buyers, pushing prices down.
- **Shifts in Supply or Demand:** Changes in factors like economic conditions, news events, or investor sentiment can shift either the supply or demand curve, leading to changes in the equilibrium price.

Examples in Action:

- **Stock Market:** A positive earnings report for a company can increase demand for its stock, pushing the price up.
- **Housing Market:** A shortage of available homes can create excess demand, leading to bidding wars and higher prices, and vice versa.
- **Commodity Markets:** A drought can reduce the supply of agricultural products, causing prices to rise.

The Nuances:

While supply and demand are fundamental, real-world markets are more complex. Other factors like market microstructure, trading costs, and investor psychology also play a role. However, understanding the basic dynamics of supply and demand provides a crucial foundation for understanding price formation and discovery.

Price Discovery Mechanisms

Think of them as the gears and levers that work behind the scenes to find that sweet spot where buyers and sellers agree.

The Basics: Supply and Demand

At the heart of price discovery is the interplay of supply and demand. When buyers are eager and sellers are hesitant, prices rise. When sellers are eager and buyers are hesitant, prices fall. The "fair" price is the point where these two forces balance out.

But how do we find that fair price? That's where different price discovery mechanisms come into play.

1. Auctions:

- **How it works:** Buyers and sellers submit their bids and asks during a specific period. At the end of the auction, all trades are executed at a single price – the price that matches the most buyers and sellers.
- **Where it's used:** Common in markets for less frequently traded assets (like some bonds or IPOs) or at the opening and closing of certain exchanges.
- **Pros:** Can be efficient for finding a fair price when there's a lot of uncertainty or limited trading activity.
- **Cons:** Less frequent trading opportunities, may not reflect real-time market conditions.

2. Continuous Trading with an Order Book:

- **How it works:** Buyers and sellers continuously submit orders to a centralized order book. The best bid and ask prices are displayed, and trades occur when a buyer's bid matches a seller's ask.
- **Where it's used:** The most common mechanism for stock exchanges and many other markets.
- **Pros:** Provides continuous liquidity, allows traders to react quickly to changing market conditions.
- **Cons:** Can be prone to volatility, especially during periods of high activity or news events.

3. Dealer Markets (Quote-Driven):

- **How it works:** Market makers (dealers) continuously quote bid and ask prices for an asset. Traders can then buy or sell from the dealer at those prices.
- **Where it's used:** Common in less liquid markets, like bond markets or certain OTC derivatives.
- **Pros:** Provides liquidity even when there are few natural buyers and sellers.
- **Cons:** Less transparent than order-driven markets, as the dealer's pricing may not fully reflect the underlying supply and demand.

The Role of Information:

Information is the lifeblood of price discovery. New information, whether it's a company earnings report or a rumor about a central bank decision, can quickly shift the balance of supply and demand, causing prices to adjust.

The Impact of Technology:

Technology has dramatically changed how price discovery happens. Electronic trading platforms, high-frequency trading algorithms, and big data analytics have made markets faster, more efficient, and more complex.

Impact of Information on Prices

Information is the lifeblood of financial markets, and it has an important role in how prices are formed and discovered. Let's explore how information impacts prices and the ripple effects it creates.

Information: The Catalyst for Change

Imagine a market as a giant puzzle where each piece represents a bit of information about an asset's value. New information, like a company earnings report, an economic announcement, or even a rumor, adds a new piece to the puzzle. This prompts investors to re-evaluate their beliefs and adjust their buying or selling decisions, causing prices to shift.

How Information Affects Prices:

- **Supply and Demand:** New information can drastically alter the balance between supply and demand. Positive news can increase demand, pushing prices up, while negative news can decrease demand, causing prices to fall.
- **Informed vs. Uninformed Traders:** Informed traders, armed with new information, will quickly adjust their trading strategies to profit from their knowledge. This can lead to rapid price changes as uninformed traders try to catch up and interpret the new information.
- **Market Efficiency:** In efficient markets, prices adjust rapidly to new information. The faster and more accurate this adjustment, the more efficient the market. This is why news releases often cause immediate price jumps.

Types of Information:

- **Fundamental Information:** This includes factors like company financials, economic indicators, and industry trends. It reflects the underlying value of an asset.
- **Technical Information:** This involves analyzing price and volume patterns to identify trends and predict future price movements.
- **Market Sentiment:** This refers to the overall mood and attitude of investors. It can be influenced by news, events, or even social media buzz.

Information Asymmetry:

When some market participants have access to information that others don't, it creates an uneven playing field. This is known as information asymmetry. Informed traders can profit from this advantage, but it can also lead to market inefficiencies and unfairness.

CHAPTER 4: MARKET LIQUIDITY

Definition and Measurement of Liquidity

It's a bit like oil in a car engine: essential for smooth operation, but not always easy to quantify.

What is Market Liquidity?

Simply put, liquidity is the ease with which you can buy or sell an asset without significantly impacting its price.

Think of it like this:

- **High Liquidity:** Imagine a bustling farmers market with tons of vendors selling the same type of apple. You can easily buy or sell a large quantity of apples without drastically changing the price.
- **Low Liquidity:** Now picture a small antique shop with a single rare vase. If you try to sell it quickly, you might have to accept a lower price than you'd like. If you try to buy a similar vase, you might have trouble finding one and end up paying a premium.

Why is Liquidity Important?

- **Price Efficiency:** Liquid markets ensure that prices accurately reflect the true value of an asset. This is because there are always enough buyers and sellers to absorb trading activity without causing large price swings.
- **Reduced Transaction Costs:** In liquid markets, the difference between the price you can buy at (ask) and the price you can sell at (bid) is narrow. This bid-ask spread represents the cost of trading, so narrower spreads mean lower costs for investors.
- **Risk Management:** Liquidity allows investors to quickly enter or exit positions, which is crucial for managing risk, especially during times of market stress. If you can't sell an asset when you need to, you could be stuck with losses.

Measuring Liquidity: Not Always Easy

Measuring liquidity isn't always straightforward. There's no single perfect metric, but here are some common approaches:

1. **Bid-Ask Spread:**
   - A narrower spread generally indicates higher liquidity.
   - However, it doesn't tell you how much you can actually trade at that price.
2. **Depth of Market (DOM):**
   - Looks at the quantity of buy and sell orders available at various price levels in the order book.
   - Deeper markets can absorb larger trades without significant price impact.
3. **Trading Volume:**
   - Measures the total number of shares or contracts traded over a given period.
   - High trading volume often suggests a liquid market, but it's not always a reliable indicator.
4. **Price Impact:**
   - Measures how much a trade moves the market price.
   - Low price impact suggests high liquidity, as large trades can be executed without causing major price disruptions.
5. **Time to Fill:**
   - Measures the time it takes for an order to be executed.
   - Faster execution times typically indicate higher liquidity.

The Importance of Context:

It's important to remember that liquidity is not a static concept. It can vary depending on:

- **Asset Class:** Large-cap stocks tend to be more liquid than small-cap stocks.
- **Time of Day:** Liquidity can be lower during pre-market or after-hours trading.
- **Market Conditions:** Volatility or market stress can significantly reduce liquidity.

Factors Affecting Liquidity

It's a complex interplay of forces, but understanding them can give you a real edge.

1. The Usual Suspects: Supply and Demand

- **Basic Economics:** The fundamental law of supply and demand is the cornerstone of liquidity. More buyers and sellers mean more potential trades, leading to greater liquidity.

- **Market Depth:** A deep market, with lots of orders at various price levels, can absorb large trades without drastic price swings. This is like a deep pool – you can jump in without making a big splash.
- **Order Imbalance:** If there's a sudden surge of buy or sell orders, it can temporarily disrupt liquidity. Imagine everyone trying to sell apples at the same time at the farmers market – prices will likely drop until balance is restored.

2. The Market Makers: Liquidity's Gatekeepers

- **Their Role:** Market makers (or liquidity providers) are the unsung heroes of liquidity. They continuously quote prices to buy and sell, ensuring there's always someone to trade with.
- **Incentives:** Market makers profit from the bid-ask spread, so they're motivated to provide liquidity. But if risks are high or profits are low, they may step back, reducing liquidity.
- **Regulation:** Regulations can impact how market makers operate, influencing their willingness to provide liquidity.

3. The Information Landscape: Knowledge is Power

- **Transparency:** When market information is readily available, investors feel more confident, leading to increased trading activity and liquidity. Think of it like a clear road map – you're more likely to drive if you know where you're going.
- **Information Asymmetry:** If some traders have an information edge over others, it can create uncertainty and reduce liquidity. This is like a poker game where you don't know the other players' cards – you're less likely to bet big.

4. The Economic Backdrop: It's All Connected

- **Economic Conditions:** A strong economy with growing corporate earnings tends to boost investor confidence and trading activity, increasing liquidity. Conversely, economic downturns or uncertainty can dry up liquidity.
- **Interest Rates:** Low-interest rates can make borrowing cheaper, encouraging investors to take on more risk and trade more actively, thus boosting liquidity.
- **Volatility:** High volatility makes markets riskier, causing some investors to pull back, reducing liquidity. This is like driving on a bumpy road – you'll slow down to avoid losing control.

5. The Trading Environment: Rules of the Game

- **Transaction Costs:** High transaction costs (commissions, fees, taxes) can deter trading activity and reduce liquidity.
- **Market Structure:** The design of the market itself (e.g., continuous trading vs. auctions, centralized exchange vs. OTC) can impact liquidity.
- **Technology:** High-speed trading algorithms can both enhance and disrupt liquidity, depending on how they're used.

6. Investor Sentiment: The X-Factor

- **Herding Behavior:** When investors follow the crowd, it can amplify market trends and create sudden surges in buying or selling, impacting liquidity.
- **Risk Aversion:** During times of uncertainty or fear, investors may hoard cash and shy away from trading, reducing liquidity.

Key Takeaways:

- Liquidity is a multi-faceted concept influenced by a wide range of factors.
- Supply and demand are the fundamental drivers of liquidity.
- Market makers are important in providing liquidity.
- Information, economic conditions, trading environment, and investor sentiment all impact liquidity.

Liquidity and Market Efficiency

These two concepts are deeply intertwined, with each influencing the other in subtle and complex ways.

What is Market Efficiency?

In a nutshell, market efficiency refers to how well prices reflect all available information.

- **Efficient Market:** Prices adjust rapidly and accurately to new information, making it difficult for anyone to consistently "beat" the market.
- **Inefficient Market:** Prices may not fully reflect available information, creating opportunities for some traders to profit at the expense of others.

The Liquidity-Efficiency Link

Think of liquidity as the grease that keeps the engine of market efficiency running smoothly. Here's how they connect:

1. **Information Flow and Price Discovery:**
   - **Liquidity's Role:** In liquid markets, a large number of buyers and sellers are actively trading. This active participation leads to a constant flow of information as traders react to news, events, and changing conditions.
   - **Efficient Price Discovery:** This information flow enables the market to quickly and accurately discover the "fair" price of an asset, ensuring that prices reflect the latest information.

2. **Arbitrage and Price Correction:**
   - **Liquidity's Role:** Liquid markets attract arbitrageurs – traders who profit from price discrepancies across different markets.
   - **Efficiency Through Arbitrage:** When a price deviates from its true value, arbitrageurs step in to buy or sell, pushing the price back in line. This process helps maintain market efficiency by ensuring that prices don't stray too far from their fundamental values.

3. **Reduced Transaction Costs:**
   - **Liquidity's Role:** Liquid markets have narrow bid-ask spreads, meaning the difference between buying and selling prices is small. This translates to lower transaction costs for investors.
   - **Efficiency Through Lower Costs:** Lower transaction costs encourage more trading activity, which in turn leads to greater information flow and more efficient price discovery.

4. **Investor Confidence and Participation:**
   - **Liquidity's Role:** Investors are more likely to participate in markets where they can easily buy or sell assets without incurring significant costs or price impact.
   - **Efficiency Through Participation:** Increased participation means a broader range of viewpoints and information being incorporated into prices, leading to more efficient markets.

The Caveats:

While liquidity is generally considered a good thing for market efficiency, there are some nuances to consider:

- **Too Much of a Good Thing?** Extremely high liquidity can sometimes lead to increased volatility, as small order imbalances can cause large price swings.
- **The Impact of High-Frequency Trading (HFT):** While HFT can contribute to liquidity, some argue that it can also create a false sense of liquidity that evaporates during times of stress.

Liquidity Risk Management

Liquidity risk is the risk that you won't be able to buy or sell an asset quickly and easily at a fair price. It's the fear that when you need to get out of a position, you'll be forced to accept a much lower price than expected or, worse, be unable to find a buyer at all.

Why Should You Care?

Liquidity risk can lead to significant financial losses, especially for large institutional investors or traders who need to execute large orders. It can also trigger a cascade of selling, exacerbating market downturns and creating systemic risk.

Types of Liquidity Risk:

1. **Market Liquidity Risk:** This is the risk that the overall market for an asset dries up, making it difficult to buy or sell at any price. This can happen during times of financial crisis or extreme market volatility.
2. **Funding Liquidity Risk:** This is the risk that you won't be able to secure the funding you need to meet your obligations, such as margin calls or collateral requirements. This can be particularly dangerous in leveraged trading strategies.

Strategies for Managing Liquidity Risk:

1. **Diversification:** Don't put all your eggs in one basket. By diversifying your portfolio across different asset classes and markets, you reduce your exposure to the liquidity risk of any single asset.
2. **Limit Orders:** Use limit orders instead of market orders. This allows you to specify the maximum price you'll pay (buy limit) or the minimum price you'll accept (sell limit), protecting you from unfavorable price movements.
3. **Liquidity Profiling:** Understand the liquidity characteristics of the assets you're trading. Some assets are inherently more liquid than others. Stocks of large, well-known companies are generally more liquid than small-cap stocks or exotic derivatives.
4. **Scenario Analysis:** Stress test your portfolio under different market scenarios. What if liquidity dries up? How would your portfolio perform? This helps you identify vulnerabilities and prepare for the worst.
5. **Contingent Funding:** Have access to backup sources of funding in case your primary source dries up. This could be a credit line with a bank or other financial institution.
6. **Monitoring Market Conditions:** Keep a close eye on market conditions and be prepared to adjust your trading strategies as liquidity conditions change.

7. **Liquidity Risk Measures:** Utilize liquidity risk measures like bid-ask spread, depth of market, and trading volume to assess the liquidity of a market or asset.
8. **Liquidity Risk Management Tools:** Many brokers and trading platforms offer tools to help you manage liquidity risk. These can include real-time monitoring of market liquidity, alerts for changes in liquidity conditions, and sophisticated order routing algorithms to access hidden liquidity.

Liquidity Provision Incentives and Obligations

These are the tools that exchanges and regulators use to encourage market makers to do their job – providing the essential lubrication that keeps markets functioning.

Incentives: The Carrot

Think of incentives as the rewards offered to market makers for providing liquidity. They come in various forms:

- **Rebates:** Cash payments to market makers for adding liquidity by posting competitive bid and ask quotes. This can be based on the volume traded or the quality of the quotes (e.g., how close they are to the mid-price).
- **Fee Reductions:** Market makers may receive discounts on trading fees, making it more profitable for them to provide liquidity.
- **Priority Access:** Some exchanges grant market makers priority access to order flow or information, giving them a competitive advantage.
- **Designated Market Maker (DMM) Programs:** These programs offer exclusive benefits to market makers, such as rebates, fee waivers, and access to special order types, in exchange for meeting specific liquidity provision obligations.

Why Incentives Matter:

- **Attract Liquidity Providers:** Incentives entice market makers to participate in the market, increasing the number of buyers and sellers available.
- **Narrow Bid-Ask Spreads:** Competition for rebates can drive market makers to post tighter spreads, reducing trading costs for investors.
- **Improve Market Quality:** Incentives can encourage market makers to provide liquidity even during volatile periods, enhancing market stability.

Obligations: The Stick

Now, let's talk about the stick: the obligations that market makers must fulfill in exchange for the incentives. These obligations are designed to ensure that market makers actually deliver on their promise of providing liquidity.

- **Quoting Requirements:** Market makers must continuously quote bid and ask prices throughout the trading day, maintaining a certain spread or depth of quotes.
- **Fill Rates:** They must execute a certain percentage of incoming orders, ensuring that traders can actually transact at the quoted prices.
- **Response Time:** Market makers must respond to incoming orders within a specified time frame, ensuring quick execution.
- **Capital Requirements:** They must maintain a certain level of capital to back their quotes and ensure they can fulfill their obligations.

Why Obligations Matter:

- **Ensure Liquidity:** Obligations hold market makers accountable for providing liquidity, preventing them from simply collecting rebates without fulfilling their role.
- **Protect Investors:** By requiring market makers to adhere to certain standards, obligations help protect investors from unfair practices and market manipulation.
- **Maintain Market Integrity:** Obligations help maintain the overall integrity of the market by ensuring that trading is fair, orderly, and transparent.

The Balancing Act:

Exchanges and regulators face a delicate balancing act when designing liquidity provision programs.

- **Too Few Incentives:** Market makers may not be motivated to provide liquidity, leading to wider spreads and reduced trading activity.
- **Too Many Incentives:** Market makers may engage in "quote stuffing" or other manipulative practices to collect rebates without actually providing meaningful liquidity.
- **Too Strict Obligations:** Market makers may be discouraged from participating, reducing competition and potentially harming market quality.
- **Too Lax Obligations:** Market makers may not fulfill their role adequately, leaving markets vulnerable to liquidity shortages and price volatility.

Liquidity provision incentives and obligations are essential tools for ensuring the smooth functioning of financial markets. By striking the right balance between rewards and responsibilities, we can create markets that are liquid, efficient, and fair for all participants.

CHAPTER 5: ORDER FLOW AND ORDER BOOK DYNAMICS

Understanding Order Flow

Let's break down the concept of order flow. Think of it as the lifeblood of the market, the constant stream of buy and sell orders that reveals the intentions and actions of market participants. Understanding order flow is like learning to read the market's mind, giving you valuable insights into where prices might be headed.

What is Order Flow?

Order flow is simply the stream of orders entering the market. It's a dynamic and ever-changing landscape, reflecting the shifting tides of supply and demand.

- **Types of Orders:** Market orders (executed immediately at the current market price) and limit orders (set a specific price at which you're willing to buy or sell).
- **Order Book:** The order book is where these orders are recorded, showing the quantity of buy and sell orders at various price levels. It's like a snapshot of the market's intentions.

Why is Order Flow Important?

1. **Reveals Market Sentiment:** By analyzing order flow, we can gauge the overall sentiment of the market. Are buyers more aggressive than sellers, or vice-versa? This can give us clues about potential price movements.
2. **Identifies Key Levels:** Order flow can help us pinpoint important support and resistance levels. These are price levels where buying or selling pressure is likely to intensify, potentially leading to reversals or breakouts.
3. **Detects Large Orders:** Order flow can reveal the presence of large institutional orders, which can have a significant impact on prices. These orders often aren't immediately visible in the order book, but their presence can be inferred from patterns in the order flow.
4. **Measures Market Strength:** By analyzing the aggressiveness of buyers and sellers (e.g., how quickly they're willing to pay up or down for an asset), we can assess the strength of a trend or potential reversal.
5. **Improves Trading Decisions:** Understanding order flow can help traders make more informed decisions about entry and exit points, stop-loss placement, and position sizing.

How to Analyze Order Flow:

- **Order Book Analysis:** Watch for changes in the size and shape of the order book. Are orders piling up at certain levels? Are there any large gaps in the book? This can indicate potential support or resistance levels.
- **Volume Analysis:** Pay attention to trading volume, especially at key price levels. High volume can confirm a breakout or reversal, while low volume may indicate a lack of conviction.
- **Time and Sales (T&S) Data:** This data shows a real-time feed of executed trades, including price, size, and direction. It can help you identify aggressive buying or selling, as well as potential hidden orders.
- **Order Flow Indicators:** Various technical indicators, like the Cumulative Delta or the Order Flow Imbalance, can help visualize order flow data and identify patterns.
- **Level 2 Data:** This data provides a more detailed view of the order book, showing individual orders and their sizes. It can be useful for identifying large orders and understanding the motivations of different market participants.

The Challenge of Order Flow Analysis:

Order flow analysis isn't easy. It requires a keen eye, experience, and the right tools. It's also important to remember that order flow is just one piece of the puzzle. Other factors like fundamental analysis, technical analysis, and market sentiment also have a role.

Structure of the Order Book

Think of it as the central command center of the market, where the intentions of buyers and sellers are laid bare. Understanding its structure is like reading a map of the market's potential movements, giving you valuable insights into price discovery and liquidity.

The Basics: Bids and Asks

At its core, the order book is a real-time record of all the active buy and sell orders for a particular security.

- **Bids (Buy Orders):** These are orders placed by traders who want to buy the security. They're organized in descending order, with the highest bid price at the top. Each bid also includes the quantity of shares or contracts the buyer wants.
- **Asks (Sell Orders):** These are orders placed by traders who want to sell the security. They're organized in ascending order, with the lowest ask price at the top. Each ask also includes the quantity the seller wants to offload.

The Bid-Ask Spread: The Market's Pulse

The difference between the best bid and the best ask is called the bid-ask spread. This spread is a key indicator of market liquidity and trading costs.

- **Narrow Spread:** A narrow spread suggests a liquid market with lots of buyers and sellers close to agreement on the price. This means you can usually buy or sell quickly without moving the market too much.
- **Wide Spread:** A wide spread indicates a less liquid market. This could mean there are fewer participants, greater uncertainty about the asset's value, or simply a temporary imbalance between buyers and sellers. Wider spreads mean higher trading costs, as you'll have to pay more to buy or accept less to sell.

Levels: The Price Tiers

The order book isn't just a jumble of bids and asks. It's organized into price levels, or tiers, where orders with the same price are grouped together.

- **Level 1:** This shows the best bid and ask prices and their corresponding quantities. It's the most basic snapshot of the market.
- **Level 2:** This gives you a deeper look into the order book, showing multiple price levels with their respective bid and ask quantities. It provides more insight into the potential supply and demand at different prices.
- **Market Depth:** The total quantity available at each price level is called market depth. A deep market has large quantities available at each price, suggesting high liquidity. A shallow market has smaller quantities, indicating lower liquidity.

Order Types and Their Placement

Different order types have different impacts on the order book:

- **Market Orders:** These execute immediately, taking out the best available price. They "eat into" the order book, potentially moving the bid or ask price.
- **Limit Orders:** These are placed within the order book at a specific price. They add to the market depth and can help narrow the spread if they are competitive with existing orders.

Order Book Dynamics: The Shifting Landscape

The order book is constantly changing as new orders are added, existing orders are cancelled or modified, and trades are executed. Watching these changes can give you valuable clues about market sentiment and potential price movements.

- **Aggressiveness:** If you see large buy orders being placed at or above the current ask price, it suggests aggressive buying pressure and a potential price increase. The opposite is true for large sell orders below the bid price.
- **Momentum:** A series of orders in one direction can create momentum, leading to further price movement in that direction.
- **Imbalance:** If there's a significant imbalance between buy and sell orders at a certain price level, it can signal a potential breakout or reversal.

Order Book Imbalances and Price Movements

Think of the order book as a scale, with buy orders on one side and sell orders on the other. When these sides are out of balance, it can tip the scales and lead to price changes. Let's explore how this works.

What is Order Book Imbalance?

Order book imbalance refers to a situation where the quantity of buy orders doesn't match the quantity of sell orders at a given price level. This creates a temporary supply and demand imbalance, which can put pressure on prices.

Types of Order Book Imbalances:

- **Bid-Side Imbalance:** This occurs when there are significantly more buy orders than sell orders at a particular price level. This creates buying pressure, pushing prices higher.
- **Ask-Side Imbalance:** This occurs when there are significantly more sell orders than buy orders at a particular price level. This creates selling pressure, driving prices lower.

How Order Book Imbalances Affect Prices:

- **Price Discovery:** Imbalances can accelerate the price discovery process. If there's a sudden surge of buy orders, it signals strong demand and encourages sellers to raise their asking prices. Conversely, a wave of sell orders signals weak demand and can lead to lower bid prices.
- **Short-Term Volatility:** Imbalances can trigger short-term price fluctuations. A large buy order can quickly consume all the available sell orders at a certain price, forcing the price higher to find new sellers. This can create a "bidding war" that pushes prices up rapidly.

- **Trend Confirmation or Reversal:** Imbalances can either confirm an existing trend or signal a potential reversal. For example, a strong bid-side imbalance during an uptrend may suggest continued buying pressure and further price increases. However, a sudden ask-side imbalance during an uptrend could be a warning sign of a potential reversal.

Factors That Influence Order Book Imbalances:

- **News and Events:** Positive or negative news about a company or the overall economy can quickly shift the balance of buy and sell orders.
- **Institutional Trading:** Large institutional investors often trade in large blocks, which can create significant imbalances in the order book.
- **Algorithmic Trading:** High-frequency trading algorithms can rapidly detect and exploit order book imbalances, contributing to short-term volatility.
- **Market Sentiment:** The overall mood of the market, whether optimistic or pessimistic, can influence the balance of buy and sell orders.

How Traders Use Order Book Imbalances:

- **Identifying Potential Trades:** Traders can use order book imbalances to identify potential entry or exit points. For example, a strong bid-side imbalance could signal a buying opportunity, while an ask-side imbalance might suggest a good time to sell.
- **Confirming Trading Signals:** Imbalances can be used to confirm other trading signals. For instance, if a technical indicator suggests a bullish trend, a strong bid-side imbalance would provide further confirmation.
- **Managing Risk:** Traders can use order book imbalances to adjust their stop-loss orders. For example, if you're long on a stock and see a large ask-side imbalance, you might tighten your stop-loss to protect your profits.

Important Considerations:

- **Imbalances are Temporary:** Order book imbalances are usually short-lived. New orders can quickly restore balance, so it's important to act quickly if you're using imbalances to make trading decisions.
- **Imbalances Can Be Misleading:** Not all imbalances lead to significant price movements. Sometimes, they can be quickly absorbed by the market. It's important to consider other factors, like market depth and overall market conditions, when interpreting order book imbalances.
- **Tools for Analyzing Order Book Imbalances:** There are various tools and software available that can help you visualize and analyze order book imbalances in real-time.

By understanding the dynamics of order book imbalances, you gain valuable insights into the forces that drive short-term price movements and can develop more effective trading strategies. However, it's important to use this information in conjunction with other forms of analysis and always be aware of the risks involved in trading.

CHAPTER 6: MARKET EFFICIENCY AND INEFFICIENCY

The Efficient Market Hypothesis

The Efficient Market Hypothesis (EMH) is a cornerstone theory in finance that has sparked countless debates and shaped investment strategies for decades. It's a bit of a controversial idea, but understanding it is crucial for anyone interested in market microstructure.

What is the Efficient Market Hypothesis (EMH)?

At its core, the EMH posits that financial markets are "informationally efficient." This means that asset prices fully reflect all available information, both public and private. The implication is that it's impossible to consistently "beat" the market by picking undervalued stocks or timing the market, since all known information is already baked into prices.

The Three Forms of EMH:

1. **Weak Form Efficiency:** Prices reflect all past market data, including historical prices and trading volume. This means technical analysis (charting) won't give you an edge, as past trends cannot predict future prices.
2. **Semi-Strong Form Efficiency:** Prices reflect all publicly available information, including financial statements, news releases, and analyst reports. This means fundamental analysis (studying a company's financials) won't help you outperform the market, as this information is already priced in.
3. **Strong Form Efficiency:** Prices reflect all information, both public and private. This means even insider information won't give you an advantage, as the market has already accounted for it.

The Implications of EMH:

- **Passive Investing:** If markets are efficient, the best strategy is to simply buy and hold a diversified portfolio of assets, tracking a broad market index. There's no point trying to pick individual stocks, as you're unlikely to outperform the market consistently.
- **The Role of Active Managers:** The EMH suggests that active fund managers who try to beat the market are essentially wasting their time (and their clients' money). Their performance, after fees, is unlikely to consistently exceed that of a passive index fund.

- **Market Pricing:** The EMH implies that prices are always "right." They may fluctuate, but these fluctuations are random and unpredictable, reflecting the arrival of new information.

Challenges to the EMH:

The EMH has been challenged on several fronts:

- **Anomalies:** Researchers have identified various market anomalies, like the small-cap effect or the momentum effect, where certain types of stocks seem to outperform others over time. These anomalies suggest that markets may not be perfectly efficient.
- **Behavioral Finance:** This field of study highlights the role of human psychology in financial markets. Behavioral biases, like overconfidence or herd behavior, can lead to irrational decision-making and market inefficiencies.
- **Limits to Arbitrage:** Even if mispricings exist, it may be difficult or costly for arbitrageurs to exploit them, allowing inefficiencies to persist.

The Reality: Somewhere in Between

Most experts agree that markets are not perfectly efficient in the strong form. Insider trading exists, and some traders may have access to information or analytical tools that others don't. However, markets are generally considered to be relatively efficient, especially in the weak and semi-strong forms.

The Bottom Line:

The Efficient Market Hypothesis is a valuable framework for understanding how markets work and the challenges of trying to beat them. While it's not a perfect theory, it highlights the importance of information in price formation and the difficulty of consistently outsmarting the market. Whether you believe in the EMH or not, understanding its principles can help you make more informed investment decisions and develop realistic expectations about market performance.

Causes of Market Inefficiency

While the Efficient Market Hypothesis (EMH) provides a useful framework, real-world markets often deviate from this ideal due to various factors. Let's explore some of the main culprits behind market inefficiency:

1. Information Asymmetry:

- **Insider Information:** When some market participants have access to non-public information that others don't, it creates an uneven playing field. This allows insiders to profit at the expense of uninformed traders, leading to mispricings.
- **Unequal Access:** Even in the absence of insider trading, not all investors have equal access to information or the resources to analyze it. This creates an information gap that can lead to inefficiencies.

2. **Transaction Costs:**
- **Commissions and Fees:** The costs associated with trading, such as brokerage commissions and exchange fees, can deter arbitrageurs from correcting mispricings. If the potential profit from a trade is smaller than the cost of executing it, the mispricing may persist.
- **Market Impact:** Large trades can move prices, creating a cost for the trader. This market impact can discourage arbitrage activity, especially for illiquid assets.

3. **Behavioral Biases:**
- **Herding Behavior:** Investors often follow the crowd, even if it means buying overpriced assets or selling undervalued ones. This herd mentality can create bubbles and crashes, leading to significant market inefficiencies.
- **Overconfidence:** Overconfident investors overestimate their ability to pick winning stocks or time the market. This can lead to excessive trading and poor investment decisions, contributing to market volatility and mispricings.
- **Loss Aversion:** Investors tend to feel the pain of losses more acutely than the pleasure of gains. This can lead them to hold onto losing investments for too long or sell winning investments too early, further distorting prices.

4. **Limits to Arbitrage:**
- **Risk and Capital Constraints:** Arbitrageurs, who theoretically should correct mispricings, face risk and capital constraints. They may not have enough capital to take large enough positions to fully correct a mispricing, or they may be unwilling to take on the risk associated with the trade.
- **Implementation Costs:** Executing arbitrage trades often involves costs, such as borrowing fees and short-selling costs. These costs can erode potential profits and make arbitrage less attractive.

5. **Market Structure:**
- **Market Fragmentation:** The fragmentation of trading across multiple venues can create liquidity pockets and information disparities, leading to price discrepancies and inefficiencies.
- **Dark Pools:** These opaque trading venues can exacerbate information asymmetry and make it difficult for prices to fully reflect all available information.

6. **Regulatory Constraints:**
- **Short-Selling Restrictions:** Regulations that limit short selling can prevent arbitrageurs from correcting overvaluations, contributing to inefficiencies.
- **Price Limits:** Price limits, which restrict how much a stock price can move in a single day, can prevent prices from adjusting fully to new information.

The Importance of Recognizing Inefficiency:

While market efficiency is a useful concept, it's important to recognize that real-world markets are often imperfect. Understanding the causes of inefficiency can help investors:

- **Identify Opportunities:** By recognizing inefficiencies, investors can potentially find undervalued assets or exploit pricing anomalies.
- **Manage Risks:** Awareness of the risks associated with inefficient markets can help investors develop more robust risk management strategies.
- **Advocate for Better Markets:** By understanding the causes of inefficiency, investors can advocate for regulatory changes or market structure improvements that promote greater fairness and efficiency.

Implications for Traders and Investors

Let's talk about the practical implications of market efficiency and inefficiency for you, the trader or investor. These concepts aren't just theoretical – they directly impact your strategies, expectations, and potential outcomes in the market.

If Markets Were Perfectly Efficient:

- **No Free Lunch:** You couldn't consistently beat the market. Prices would always reflect all available information, leaving no room for easy profits.
- **Passive Investing Wins:** The best strategy would be to buy and hold a diversified portfolio that tracks the overall market. Trying to pick individual stocks or time the market would be futile.
- **Active Management Under Scrutiny:** Active fund managers would struggle to justify their fees, as their performance would be unlikely to consistently outperform a passive index fund.
- **Focus on Costs:** Since outperforming the market would be difficult, investors would focus on minimizing trading costs and taxes to maximize their returns.

But Markets Aren't Always Perfectly Efficient:

- **Opportunities for Active Traders:** Inefficiencies create opportunities for skilled traders to profit. They can exploit mispricings caused by information asymmetry, behavioral biases, or market structure limitations.
- **The Value of Information:** Information becomes a valuable commodity. Those with access to unique insights or superior analytical tools can potentially gain an edge over the market.
- **Risk Management is Key:** Market inefficiencies can lead to increased volatility and unexpected price movements. Prudent risk management becomes crucial to protect your capital from sudden losses.

Implications for Different Types of Traders and Investors:

- **Long-Term Investors:** Even if markets aren't perfectly efficient, long-term investors can still benefit from diversification and a disciplined approach. They can take advantage of market downturns to buy assets at lower prices and focus on companies with strong fundamentals and long-term growth potential.
- **Short-Term Traders:** Traders who focus on short-term price movements can potentially profit from market inefficiencies. They can use technical analysis, order flow analysis, or other tools to identify mispricings and exploit them. However, this approach requires skill, experience, and a deep understanding of market microstructure.
- **Arbitrageurs:** These specialized traders seek to profit from price discrepancies across different markets or securities. They have an important role in correcting inefficiencies, but their strategies can be complex and risky.
- **Institutional Investors:** Large institutional investors often have the resources to conduct in-depth research and analysis, giving them a potential advantage in identifying inefficiencies. However, they also face challenges like market impact, where their large trades can move prices against them.
- **Retail Investors:** Individual investors often have limited resources and may be more susceptible to behavioral biases. However, they can still benefit from understanding market efficiency and inefficiency and making informed decisions based on their risk tolerance and investment goals.

The Importance of Adaptability:

Market conditions are constantly changing. What may be an inefficient market today could become more efficient tomorrow due to increased information flow, technological advancements, or regulatory changes. Successful traders and investors are adaptable and continuously adjust their strategies to the prevailing market conditions.

Anomalies and Patterns

These are the curious phenomena that sometimes defy the Efficient Market Hypothesis (EMH), suggesting that markets aren't always perfectly rational and predictable. Understanding these anomalies can shed light on potential inefficiencies and offer valuable insights for traders and investors.

What are Market Anomalies?

Market anomalies are patterns in asset prices or returns that seem to contradict the EMH, which posits that prices should fully reflect all available information. They are often recurring patterns that can be exploited for potential profit, but they also raise questions about market efficiency and the underlying causes of these deviations.

Types of Market Anomalies:

1. **Calendar Anomalies:**
   - **January Effect:** The tendency for stock prices to rise abnormally in January, often attributed to tax-loss selling in December and subsequent buying in the new year.
   - **Turn-of-the-Month Effect:** Higher returns are often observed in the days surrounding the turn of the month, possibly due to increased fund flows or portfolio rebalancing.
   - **Day-of-the-Week Effect:** Certain days of the week, like Monday or Friday, may exhibit different average returns than other days, potentially due to investor behavior or trading patterns.

2. **Value Anomalies:**
   - **Value Effect:** Stocks with lower valuations (e.g., low price-to-earnings or price-to-book ratios) tend to outperform stocks with higher valuations over the long term. This suggests that the market may not always price stocks accurately based on their fundamental value.
   - **Size Effect:** Smaller-cap stocks have historically outperformed large-cap stocks, although this effect has been less pronounced in recent years. This could be due to higher risk associated with smaller companies or potential mispricings.

3. **Momentum Anomalies:**
   - **Momentum Effect:** Stocks that have recently performed well tend to continue outperforming, while stocks that have performed poorly tend to continue underperforming. This suggests that trends can persist in the market, contradicting the EMH's notion of random price movements.

4. **Other Anomalies:**

- **Post-Earnings Announcement Drift (PEAD):** Stock prices tend to continue moving in the direction of an earnings surprise (positive or negative) for some time after the announcement. This suggests that the market may not fully and immediately incorporate earnings information into prices. This has to do with the divergence between systematic strategies (which react more or less instantly) and discretionary strategies (which require human input and are slower).
- **Volatility Anomalies:** Low-volatility stocks tend to outperform high-volatility stocks over the long term, even after adjusting for risk. This challenges the traditional risk-return tradeoff and suggests that investors may overpay for volatile stocks.

Explaining Market Anomalies:

The causes of market anomalies are debated among academics and practitioners. Some possible explanations include:

- **Behavioral Biases:** Investor irrationality, such as overreaction to news or herding behavior, can create and sustain anomalies.
- **Risk Factors:** Anomalies may reflect hidden risk factors that are not fully captured by traditional models.
- **Market Microstructure Effects:** The mechanics of trading, such as transaction costs and liquidity constraints, can create temporary price deviations that lead to anomalies.

Implications for Traders and Investors:

- **Exploiting Anomalies:** Some traders actively seek to exploit market anomalies through strategies like momentum trading or value investing.
- **Risk Management:** Investors should be aware of anomalies when constructing portfolios and consider the potential impact of these patterns on their investments.
- **The Efficient Market Debate:** The existence of anomalies challenges the idea that markets are always perfectly efficient and suggests that opportunities for excess returns may exist, even if they are difficult to consistently exploit.

Limits to Arbitrage

In an ideal world, arbitrage is a riskless profit opportunity. If the same asset trades at different prices in two markets, a trader can buy low in one market and sell high in the other, pocketing the difference. This buying and selling pressure should theoretically push prices back in line, eliminating the mispricing.

The Reality: Limits to Arbitrage

The real world, however, is not so simple. Several factors can limit the effectiveness of arbitrage:

- **Transaction Costs:** Brokerage commissions, exchange fees, and other trading costs can eat into potential arbitrage profits, making some trades unprofitable.
- **Market Impact:** Large arbitrage trades can move prices, working against the arbitrageur. This is especially true in less liquid markets where it's harder to buy or sell large quantities without impacting prices.
- **Risk:** Arbitrage is not always risk-free. Prices can move further away from their fair value before converging, leading to losses for the arbitrageur.
- **Capital Constraints:** Arbitrageurs need capital to exploit mispricings. Limited capital restricts the size of their trades and their ability to fully correct market inefficiencies.
- **Fundamental Risk:** The underlying asset may change in value while the arbitrage trade is in progress, leading to unexpected losses.
- **Noise Trader Risk:** Irrational traders can push prices further away from their fundamental value, making it difficult for arbitrageurs to profit.
- **Implementation Constraints:** Some arbitrage strategies, like short selling, may be restricted by regulation or market conditions, limiting their effectiveness.

The Implications:

The existence of limits to arbitrage means that mispricings can persist for extended periods. This has several important implications:

- **Market Inefficiency:** It challenges the notion of perfectly efficient markets, as prices may not always reflect all available information.
- **Opportunities for Active Traders:** Savvy traders who can identify and exploit mispricings can potentially earn excess returns.
- **Increased Volatility:** Limits to arbitrage can contribute to market volatility, as prices may overreact to news or events and take longer to adjust back to their fair value.

While arbitrage plays an important role in keeping markets efficient, its effectiveness is not unlimited. Understanding the limits to arbitrage is vital for comprehending why mispricings can occur and persist in financial markets.

CHAPTER 7: THE ROLE OF MARKET MAKERS

Functions and Responsibilities

These key players keep the gears turning, ensuring that you can buy or sell an asset when you need to, even if there's no one else on the other side of the trade.

The Market Maker's Job Description:

1. **Providing Liquidity:** This is their core function. Market makers continuously quote both bid (the price they'll buy at) and ask (the price they'll sell at) prices for a security. This creates a two-sided market where you can always find a buyer or seller, even when natural supply and demand are imbalanced.
2. **Narrowing Spreads:** By competing with each other to offer the best prices, market makers help keep the bid-ask spread tight. This spread represents the cost of trading, so narrower spreads benefit investors.
3. **Facilitating Price Discovery:** The quotes provided by market makers help the market discover the "fair" price of an asset. Their actions reflect their assessment of the security's value based on information and risk factors.
4. **Stabilizing Prices:** Market makers act as shock absorbers during volatile times. They step in to buy when others are selling, and sell when others are buying, helping to prevent extreme price swings.
5. **Managing Inventory:** Market makers hold inventory of the securities they trade. They adjust their bid and ask prices to manage this inventory and maintain a balanced book.

Responsibilities of Market Makers:

- **Continuous Quoting:** They must continuously quote prices throughout the trading day, even during periods of low activity or high volatility.
- **Orderly Markets:** They are expected to maintain orderly markets by preventing excessive price swings and ensuring smooth trading.
- **Fairness and Transparency:** They must adhere to strict regulations to prevent market manipulation and ensure fair treatment of all market participants.
- **Capital Requirements:** They need to maintain sufficient capital to back their quotes and meet their trading obligations.

Why Market Makers Matter:

Market makers are vital in ensuring the smooth functioning of financial markets. Their presence increases liquidity, reduces trading costs, and enhances price discovery. They are particularly important in less liquid markets, like bond markets or markets for smaller stocks, where natural buyers and sellers may be scarce.

The Changing Landscape:

The role of market makers is evolving with the rise of electronic trading and high-frequency trading (HFT). HFT firms now provide a significant portion of liquidity in many markets, competing with traditional market makers. This has led to increased efficiency and tighter spreads, but also raises questions about the impact of HFT on market stability and fairness.

How Market Makers Influence Liquidity

Market makers are like the lifeguards of liquidity. They ensure that trading happens smoothly, even when the waves of supply and demand get a little choppy. Let's break down how they exert their influence:

1. **Providing a Two-Sided Market:**

Market makers constantly offer to buy (bid) and sell (ask) a security at publicly quoted prices. This means there's always a counterparty available for you to trade with, even if there are no other willing buyers or sellers at that moment. This availability is the very definition of liquidity.

2. **Narrowing Bid-Ask Spreads:**

Market makers compete with each other to provide the best prices. This competition drives down the difference between the bid and ask price (the spread), which is the implicit cost you pay for trading. Narrower spreads mean lower transaction costs and better prices for you.

3. **Absorbing Order Imbalances:**

When there's a surge of buy or sell orders, market makers step in to take the other side of the trade. This prevents prices from swinging wildly and ensures that markets remain orderly. Think of them as shock absorbers for the market.

4. **Stabilizing Prices During Volatility:**

During volatile times, when prices are bouncing around, market makers can help calm the waters. By providing a consistent presence and absorbing excess volatility, they create a more stable trading environment.

5. Enhancing Price Discovery:

Market makers' quotes reflect their assessment of a security's fair value, based on their analysis of available information. Their actions help the market converge on a price that reflects the consensus view of all participants. This is essential for price efficiency.

The Market Maker's Toolkit:

- **Inventory Management:** They actively manage their inventory of the securities they trade, adjusting bid and ask prices to maintain a balanced position.
- **Risk Management:** They employ sophisticated risk management strategies to protect themselves from adverse price movements.
- **Technology:** They use advanced algorithms and high-speed trading systems to analyze market data, execute trades, and manage their risk.

Key Takeaway:

Market makers are essential for maintaining healthy and efficient markets. They provide the liquidity that allows you to trade when you want, at a fair price. They act as shock absorbers during volatile times, and their actions contribute to accurate price discovery.

Risks and Challenges Faced by Market Makers

While they are vital in the financial ecosystem, they also face a unique set of risks and challenges that can make their job quite demanding.

1. Inventory Risk:

Imagine holding a bunch of apples that you need to sell. If the price of apples suddenly drops, you're stuck with a loss. Market makers face a similar risk. They hold inventory of securities, and if prices move against them, they can lose money.

2. Adverse Selection Risk:

This is the risk of trading with someone who has better information than you. Informed traders can pick off market makers' quotes, leaving them with unfavorable positions. Think of it like a poker game where you keep getting dealt bad hands.

3. Information Risk:

Market conditions can change rapidly due to news events, economic data, or even rumors. Market makers need to constantly stay on top of the latest information to adjust their quotes and avoid losses.

4. Technology Risk:

Market makers rely heavily on technology for order execution and risk management. Technical glitches, system failures, or cyberattacks can disrupt their operations and lead to significant losses.

5. Regulatory Risk:

Market makers operate in a heavily regulated environment. Changes in regulations, like stricter capital requirements or restrictions on certain trading practices, can impact their profitability and business models.

6. Competition:

The rise of high-frequency trading (HFT) has intensified competition among market makers. HFT firms, with their speed and sophisticated algorithms, can quickly react to market changes and scoop up profitable opportunities, leaving traditional market makers with slimmer margins.

7. Market Volatility:

Periods of high market volatility can be particularly challenging for market makers. Wide price swings can lead to increased inventory risk and make it difficult to manage risk effectively.

8. Capital Constraints:

Market makers need sufficient capital to back their quotes and meet their trading obligations. During times of stress, they may face difficulty accessing funding, which can limit their ability to provide liquidity.

How Market Makers Mitigate Risks:

- **Risk Management Systems:** They employ sophisticated risk models and trading algorithms to monitor their positions and manage risk in real-time.
- **Diversification:** They trade a wide range of securities to spread out their risk.
- **Hedging:** They use hedging strategies, like options or futures, to offset potential losses from adverse price movements.
- **Technology:** They invest heavily in technology to gain a competitive edge and ensure reliable and efficient trading operations.

Market Making Obligations and Privileges

Let's look into the quid pro quo of market making: the obligations they must fulfill and the privileges they enjoy in return. It's a balancing act that ensures market makers provide the liquidity markets need while allowing them to profit from their role.

Market Making Obligations:

- **Continuous Quoting:** Market makers are required to maintain continuous two-sided quotes (bid and ask) for designated securities throughout the trading day. This ensures there's always a buyer and seller available, even during lulls or volatile periods.
- **Minimum Quote Sizes:** They must offer to trade a minimum number of shares or contracts at their quoted prices, providing a certain level of depth to the market.
- **Maximum Spread:** The difference between their bid and ask prices (the spread) is often regulated, ensuring they don't take excessive advantage of their position.
- **Fill Rates:** They're expected to execute a certain percentage of incoming orders, ensuring they're not just posting quotes but actually facilitating trades.
- **Response Time:** They must respond to orders quickly, contributing to the market's overall speed and efficiency.
- **Capital Requirements:** Market makers must hold a certain amount of capital to back their quotes, ensuring they can fulfill their trading obligations.

Market Making Privileges:

- **Rebates and Fee Reductions:** Exchanges often offer financial incentives like rebates (payments for providing liquidity) or reduced trading fees to market makers. This compensates them for the risks they take and the costs they incur.
- **Priority Access:** Market makers may receive preferential access to order flow or information, giving them a slight edge in trading.

- **Designated Market Maker (DMM) Status:** On some exchanges, market makers with a proven track record can become designated market makers (DMMs). This special status comes with additional benefits, like even larger rebates or exclusive access to certain order types.

Why the Balance Matters:

- **Too Many Obligations:** Overly burdensome obligations can discourage market makers from participating, reducing liquidity and widening spreads.
- **Too Many Privileges:** Excessive perks can lead to complacency or even market manipulation, where market makers focus on maximizing rebates rather than providing genuine liquidity.

Striking the Right Balance:

Exchanges and regulators constantly fine-tune the balance between obligations and privileges. The goal is to create an environment where market makers are incentivized to provide liquidity while still ensuring fair and orderly markets for all participants.

Inventory Risk Management by Market Makers

Inventory risk management is one of the biggest challenges faced by market makers. It's a bit like juggling chainsaws: exciting, but potentially dangerous if not handled carefully.

The Inventory Tightrope

Market makers are in the business of buying and selling assets. To do this, they need to hold inventory of the securities they trade. But holding inventory exposes them to risk:

- **Price Risk:** If the price of an asset falls after the market maker buys it, they're sitting on a potential loss. This is especially true in volatile markets where prices can swing wildly.
- **Inventory Imbalance:** If a market maker accumulates too much of one asset (e.g., too many shares of a particular stock), it can become difficult to unload that position without significantly impacting the market price.

Inventory Risk Management Strategies

Market makers use a variety of strategies to mitigate inventory risk:

1. **Dynamic Hedging:** They offset their exposure to price risk by taking opposite positions in related markets. For example, a market maker who buys a stock might simultaneously sell a call option on that stock to protect against a price increase.
2. **Adjusting Quotes:** They constantly monitor market conditions and adjust their bid and ask prices to attract or discourage trading based on their inventory position. If they're long on a stock, they might lower their bid price to encourage buying.
3. **Spreading Risk:** They trade a diverse range of securities to avoid excessive concentration in any single asset.
4. **Liquidity Management:** They actively manage their cash and other liquid assets to ensure they can meet their financial obligations and cover potential losses.
5. **Risk Limits:** They set internal limits on the amount of inventory they can hold, the maximum position size for any single trade, and the overall risk they're willing to take.

The Impact of Technology

Technology has revolutionized inventory risk management for market makers. Sophisticated algorithms and high-speed trading systems allow them to monitor market conditions, adjust quotes, and execute trades at lightning-fast speeds. This has made it possible to manage risk more effectively, but it has also increased the complexity and potential for technological failures.

The Importance of Inventory Risk Management

Effective inventory risk management is crucial for market makers to survive and thrive. It allows them to provide liquidity to the market while protecting their own capital. This ultimately benefits all market participants by ensuring a smooth and orderly trading environment.

CHAPTER 8: TRADING STRATEGIES

Market Making Strategies

Let's explore some common market-making strategies:

1. Basic Market Making:

- **The Core Idea:** This is the bread and butter of market making. It involves continuously quoting both bid and ask prices for a security, aiming to capture the spread (the difference between the two) as profit.
- **The Strategy:** Market makers adjust their quotes based on market conditions, their inventory position, and their risk appetite. They try to balance buying and selling pressure to avoid accumulating too much inventory and manage their exposure to price risk.
- **Key Considerations:** This strategy requires careful monitoring of market data, quick decision-making, and effective risk management tools.

2. Inventory-Based Market Making:

- **The Core Idea:** This strategy focuses on managing the market maker's inventory of the security they're trading. The goal is to avoid getting stuck with too much inventory, which could lead to losses if the price moves against them.
- **The Strategy:** Market makers adjust their quotes to incentivize buying or selling depending on their inventory level. For example, if they're long on a stock, they might lower their bid price to encourage buying.
- **Key Considerations:** This strategy requires accurate inventory tracking and a deep understanding of supply and demand dynamics.

3. Information-Based Market Making:

- **The Core Idea:** This strategy involves incorporating information about the asset's fundamental value or potential future price movements into the quoting process.
- **The Strategy:** Market makers may adjust their quotes based on news, analyst reports, or other information that could impact the security's value. They might also use predictive models to anticipate price movements.
- **Key Considerations:** This strategy requires access to high-quality information and the ability to analyze it quickly and accurately.

4. Liquidity-Driven Market Making:

- **The Core Idea:** This strategy prioritizes providing liquidity to the market, even if it means sacrificing some potential profit. The goal is to build a reputation as a reliable liquidity provider and attract more order flow over the long term.
- **The Strategy:** Market makers may offer tighter spreads or larger quote sizes than they would otherwise, even if it means accepting lower profits on individual trades.
- **Key Considerations:** This strategy can be effective in building relationships with institutional investors and gaining access to lucrative order flow, but it requires a long-term perspective and a willingness to forgo short-term gains.

5. Statistical Arbitrage Market Making:

- **The Core Idea:** This strategy combines market making with statistical arbitrage, which involves exploiting temporary price discrepancies between related securities.
- **The Strategy:** Market makers use statistical models to identify mispricings and then adjust their quotes to profit from the expected price convergence.
- **Key Considerations:** This strategy requires sophisticated modeling and risk management capabilities, as well as access to real-time market data.

Key Takeaways:

- Market making is not a passive activity. It involves active decision-making and risk management.
- Market makers use a variety of strategies, depending on market conditions, their inventory position, and their risk appetite.
- Technology plays a crucial role in market making, enabling faster execution and more sophisticated risk management.
- Understanding market-making strategies can provide valuable insights into how prices are formed and how markets function.

Arbitrage and Statistical Arbitrage

These strategies exploit market inefficiencies to generate profits, and they're closely tied to the concepts we've been exploring in market microstructure.

Arbitrage: The Risk-Free Profit

- **The Concept:** Arbitrage is the simultaneous buying and selling of the same asset (or equivalent assets) in different markets to profit from price discrepancies. The classic example is buying a stock on one exchange where

it's cheaper and simultaneously selling it on another exchange where it's more expensive.
- **The Goal:** To lock in a risk-free profit by exploiting temporary price differences.
- **The Challenges:**
  - **Speed:** Arbitrage opportunities often disappear quickly as other traders pounce on them. You need to be fast to capitalize.
  - **Transaction Costs:** Commissions, fees, and other trading costs can eat into your profits, so you need to factor them in when calculating potential gains.
  - **Market Impact:** Large arbitrage trades can move prices, potentially eroding your profit margin.

Types of Arbitrage:

- **Pure Arbitrage:** This involves trading identical assets with no risk. It's rare in practice, as most arbitrage opportunities involve some degree of risk.
- **Merger Arbitrage:** This involves buying the stock of a company being acquired and selling short the stock of the acquiring company. The profit potential comes from the spread between the offer price and the current market price.
- **Convertible Arbitrage:** This involves buying a convertible bond (a bond that can be converted into stock) and short selling the underlying stock. The profit potential comes from the difference in prices and interest rate differentials.
- **Statistical Arbitrage:** This is a more complex form of arbitrage that we'll discuss in more detail below.

Statistical Arbitrage: Finding Patterns in the Noise

- **The Concept:** Statistical arbitrage (Stat Arb) involves using statistical models and algorithms to identify and exploit pricing anomalies or temporary mispricings in related securities. It's not a risk-free strategy, as it relies on statistical predictions rather than guaranteed price differences.
- **The Goal:** To generate profits from small, but statistically significant, price discrepancies that are expected to revert to their mean.
- **The Challenges:**
  - **Model Risk:** If your model is flawed, you could make incorrect predictions and lose money.
  - **Market Risk:** Sudden market events can disrupt expected price patterns, leading to losses.
  - **Overcrowding:** If too many traders are using the same strategy, it can become less effective as the mispricing is corrected.

Types of Statistical Arbitrage Strategies:

- **Pairs Trading:** Identifying pairs of stocks that are historically correlated and trading them when their prices diverge, expecting them to eventually converge again.
- **Mean Reversion:** Betting on the idea that prices that have deviated significantly from their historical average will eventually revert back to the mean.
- **Index Arbitrage:** Exploiting price differences between a stock index and the underlying stocks that make up the index.

How Arbitrage and Stat Arb Influence Market Microstructure:

- **Price Efficiency:** Arbitrageurs and stat arb traders help keep markets efficient by correcting mispricings and ensuring that prices reflect all available information.
- **Liquidity:** Their trading activity provides liquidity to the market, making it easier for other participants to buy and sell.
- **Volatility:** While they can help reduce volatility by correcting mispricings, their actions can also contribute to short-term volatility as they enter and exit positions.

Algorithmic and High-Frequency Trading

Let's talk about the speedsters of the trading world: algorithmic trading (AT) and its turbocharged cousin, high-frequency trading (HFT). These strategies harness the power of computers and data to execute trades at lightning speed, often leaving human traders in the dust.

Algorithmic Trading (AT): The Rise of the Machines

- **What it is:** Using computer programs to make trading decisions and automatically execute orders based on pre-defined rules. It's like having a tireless robot trader working for you 24/7.
- **How it works:** Algorithms analyze market data, identify trading opportunities, and generate buy or sell signals. Once a signal is triggered, the algorithm automatically executes the trade.
- **Why it's used:**
  - **Speed:** Algorithms can react to market changes much faster than humans, allowing them to capture fleeting opportunities.
  - **Consistency:** They eliminate human emotions and biases from trading, leading to more disciplined execution.
  - **Scalability:** They can handle a large number of trades simultaneously across different markets.

Types of Algorithmic Trading Strategies:

- **Trend Following:** Algorithms that identify and follow trends in price or other market data.
- **Mean Reversion:** Algorithms that bet on prices reverting to their average after deviating significantly.
- **Arbitrage:** Algorithms that exploit price differences between related securities or markets.
- **Market Making:** Algorithms that provide liquidity by continuously quoting bid and ask prices.

High-Frequency Trading (HFT): The Need for Speed

- **What it is:** A subset of algorithmic trading that focuses on extremely rapid trading, with holding periods often measured in milliseconds or even microseconds.
- **How it works:** HFT firms use powerful computers, co-located servers near exchanges, and ultra-low latency connections to gain a speed advantage over other traders.
- **Why it's used:**
  - **Capturing Tiny Profits:** HFT strategies aim to profit from small price discrepancies that exist for very short periods.
  - **Providing Liquidity:** Some HFT firms act as market makers, providing liquidity to the market and earning rebates from exchanges.
  - **Arbitrage:** HFT algorithms can quickly identify and exploit arbitrage opportunities across different markets or securities.

The Impact of AT and HFT on Market Microstructure:

- **Increased Liquidity:** AT and HFT have significantly increased liquidity in many markets, making it easier and faster to trade.
- **Reduced Trading Costs:** Competition among HFT firms has narrowed bid-ask spreads, lowering transaction costs for investors.
- **Increased Volatility:** The speed and volume of AT and HFT can amplify market volatility, especially during periods of stress.
- **Flash Crashes:** HFT has been implicated in several flash crashes, where prices plummet rapidly and then recover just as quickly.
- **Market Fragmentation:** HFT has contributed to the fragmentation of markets, as firms seek to trade on multiple venues to gain a speed advantage.
- **Arms Race in Technology:** The quest for speed has led to an arms race in technology, with firms investing heavily in faster hardware, software, and data feeds.

The Controversies Surrounding HFT:

- **Fairness:** Some argue that HFT gives certain firms an unfair advantage due to their technological prowess and access to high-speed data feeds.
- **Market Stability:** Concerns have been raised that HFT can exacerbate market volatility and contribute to flash crashes.
- **Predatory Practices:** Some HFT strategies, like spoofing (placing orders with no intention of executing them), have been criticized as manipulative.

News-Based and Event-Driven Strategies

These strategies revolve around the idea that news and events – from company earnings reports to geopolitical developments – can significantly impact market prices. Traders who employ these strategies aim to profit from the short-term volatility and price movements caused by such events.

News-Based Trading:

- **The Core Idea:** This strategy involves reacting quickly to news releases and market-moving events. Traders who use this strategy believe that they can gain an edge by being among the first to act on new information.
- **The Process:**
  - **Monitoring News Feeds:** Traders constantly monitor news sources, social media, and other channels for relevant information.
  - **Analyzing Information:** They quickly assess the potential impact of the news on the market and the specific securities they're interested in.
  - **Executing Trades:** They swiftly enter or exit positions based on their analysis, aiming to profit from the anticipated price movements.
- **Key Considerations:**
  - **Speed and Efficiency:** News-based trading requires lightning-fast execution. Traders often use algorithmic trading systems to automate their trades and react to news in milliseconds.
  - **Information Accuracy:** The quality and reliability of information are crucial. False or misleading news can lead to costly mistakes.
  - **Risk Management:** News-based trading can be highly volatile. Traders need to carefully manage their risk by setting stop-loss orders and position sizing appropriately.

Event-Driven Trading:

- **The Core Idea:** This strategy focuses on specific events that are expected to have a significant impact on a company's stock price or the broader market. These events can be company-specific (like earnings announcements or mergers) or macroeconomic (like interest rate decisions or political events).

- **The Process:**
  - **Identifying Events:** Traders research and identify upcoming events that could trigger price movements.
  - **Analyzing the Potential Impact:** They assess the likely direction and magnitude of the price movement based on the nature of the event and market conditions.
  - **Formulating a Trading Plan:** They develop a detailed plan, including entry and exit points, stop-loss orders, and position sizing.
  - **Executing the Trade:** They implement their plan when the event occurs, aiming to profit from the anticipated price movement.
- **Key Considerations:**
  - **Thorough Research:** Event-driven trading requires in-depth research and analysis to understand the potential impact of different events on specific securities.
  - **Timing and Execution:** Proper timing is crucial. Traders need to enter and exit positions at the right time to maximize profits and minimize losses.
  - **Risk Management:** Event-driven trading carries unique risks, such as unexpected news or outcomes. Traders need to be prepared for surprises and have risk mitigation strategies in place.

Types of Event-Driven Strategies:

- **Earnings Announcements:** Traders bet on the direction of a company's stock price after its earnings report is released.
- **Mergers and Acquisitions:** Traders speculate on the impact of mergers and acquisitions on the stock prices of the companies involved.
- **Spin-offs and Divestitures:** Traders try to profit from the price movements of companies that are being spun off or divested.
- **Regulatory Changes:** Traders anticipate how regulatory changes, such as new laws or policies, will affect specific industries or sectors.
- **Economic Data Releases:** Traders react to economic data releases, such as GDP growth, inflation, or employment figures, which can influence market sentiment and asset prices.

Execution Strategies and Algorithms

Think of trying to buy 10,000 shares of a company all at once. You'd probably push the price up against yourself before you could fill the entire order. Execution strategies help you avoid this "market impact" by breaking your order into smaller chunks and strategically timing their release.

Types of Execution Strategies

1. **Time-Weighted Average Price (TWAP):**
   - **The Goal:** Execute your order evenly over a specified period to achieve the average market price.
   - **The Method:** Divide your order into smaller slices and execute them at regular intervals.
   - **Best for:** Large orders in relatively liquid markets where you're not too worried about short-term price fluctuations.
2. **Volume-Weighted Average Price (VWAP):**
   - **The Goal:** Execute your order in line with the volume patterns of the market.
   - **The Method:** Break up your order and trade more aggressively when volume is high, and less aggressively when volume is low.
   - **Best for:** Orders where you want to minimize market impact and blend in with the natural flow of trading.
3. **Implementation Shortfall (IS):**
   - **The Goal:** Minimize the difference between the price you *wanted* to get and the price you *actually* get.
   - **The Method:** Incorporates both the explicit costs (commissions, fees) and the implicit costs (market impact) of trading into the decision-making process.
   - **Best for:** Large institutional orders where market impact is a major concern.
4. **Percent of Volume (POV):**
   - **The Goal:** Trade a certain percentage of the total market volume over a specified period.
   - **The Method:** Adjust the size of your orders based on the current trading volume.
   - **Best for:** Orders where you want to maintain a consistent presence in the market without overwhelming it.
5. **Other Strategies:**
   - **Market on Close (MOC):** Execute your order at the closing price of the market.
   - **Pegged Orders:** Set your order relative to the best bid or ask price (e.g., "buy 100 shares 5 cents above the current ask").
   - **Iceberg Orders:** Only display a small portion of your order in the market, with the rest hidden from view.

Execution Algorithms: The Brains Behind the Trades

Execution algorithms are the computer programs that carry out these strategies. They use complex logic and real-time market data to make split-second decisions about when and how to trade.

- **Key Components:**

- **Order Placement Logic:** Determines the timing and size of individual orders.
- **Routing Logic:** Decides which trading venues to send orders to.
- **Price/Volume Forecasting:** Uses predictive models to anticipate market movements and optimize execution.

Choosing the Right Strategy and Algorithm

The best execution strategy and algorithm depend on various factors:

- **Order Size:** Large orders typically require more sophisticated strategies to minimize market impact.
- **Market Conditions:** Volatile markets may require different strategies than stable ones.
- **Urgency:** If you need to execute quickly, a market order might be best, but it could come at the cost of a less favorable price.
- **Risk Tolerance:** Some strategies are riskier than others (e.g., high-frequency trading).

The Bottom Line

Execution strategies and algorithms are essential tools in the modern trading world. They allow traders to navigate complex markets, minimize transaction costs, and achieve their investment goals. By understanding these tools and how they work, you can make more informed decisions about how to execute your trades and gain a competitive edge in the market.

CHAPTER 9: BEHAVIORAL ASPECTS OF TRADING

Psychology of Traders and Investors

This is where the rubber meets the road in market microstructure – where human emotions and biases collide with cold, hard data and rational decision-making. Understanding this psychological aspect is key to grasping why markets don't always behave as the Efficient Market Hypothesis (EMH) suggests.

The Emotional Rollercoaster

Traders and investors are not emotionless robots. We're all human, and our decisions are often influenced by a complex cocktail of emotions:

- **Fear:** The fear of missing out (FOMO) can lead to impulsive buying, while the fear of loss can cause panic selling.
- **Greed:** The desire for quick riches can drive excessive risk-taking and overconfidence.
- **Hope:** The hope of recovering losses can lead to doubling down on losing positions, ignoring clear warning signs.
- **Regret:** The pain of making a wrong decision can lead to hesitation and missed opportunities.

These emotions can cloud our judgment, distort our perception of risk, and lead us to make irrational decisions that deviate from sound investment principles.

Behavioral Biases: The Mind's Shortcuts

To cope with the complexity of financial markets, our brains often rely on mental shortcuts called heuristics. These shortcuts can be useful in everyday life, but in the world of investing, they can lead to systematic errors in judgment, known as behavioral biases.

- **Overconfidence:** We tend to overestimate our abilities and the accuracy of our predictions. This can lead to excessive trading and underestimating risk.
- **Anchoring:** We tend to latch onto an initial piece of information (like a stock's purchase price) and give it too much weight in our decision-making. This can prevent us from adjusting our views when new information emerges.
- **Confirmation Bias:** We tend to seek out information that confirms our existing beliefs and ignore evidence that contradicts them. This can lead to tunnel vision and prevent us from seeing the full picture.

- **Loss Aversion:** We feel the pain of losses more acutely than the pleasure of gains. This can make us hold onto losing investments for too long or sell winning investments too early.
- **Herding:** We tend to follow the crowd, even if it means ignoring our own analysis or judgment. This can lead to asset bubbles and crashes.

The Impact on Market Microstructure:

These psychological factors can significantly impact market microstructure:

- **Price Volatility:** Emotional trading and behavioral biases can amplify price swings, creating opportunities for some traders but also increasing risk for others.
- **Trading Volume:** Overconfidence and herding behavior can lead to excessive trading, increasing volume but not necessarily improving market efficiency.
- **Liquidity:** Panic selling or a reluctance to trade due to fear can reduce liquidity, making it harder to buy or sell assets at fair prices.
- **Market Anomalies:** Behavioral biases can contribute to market anomalies, like the January effect or the momentum effect, where prices deviate from what traditional finance theory would predict.

Strategies for Overcoming Biases:

- **Self-Awareness:** Recognize that you're not immune to emotions and biases.
- **Education:** Learn about behavioral finance and the common pitfalls that investors fall into.
- **Discipline:** Develop a trading plan and stick to it, even when emotions run high.
- **Diversification:** Spread your investments across different asset classes to reduce risk.
- **Seek Advice:** Consult with a financial advisor or mentor who can provide a different perspective.

Behavioral Biases in Trading

These mental shortcuts and quirks in our thinking can lead to irrational decisions that can cost us dearly in the financial arena. Understanding these biases is key to making better, more informed choices.

1. Overconfidence Bias:

- **The Trap:** We tend to overestimate our abilities and the accuracy of our predictions. This can lead to excessive trading, underestimating risk, and holding onto losing positions for too long.
- **Example:** A trader who has made a few successful trades might start believing they have a "hot hand" and take on increasingly risky bets.

2. Loss Aversion Bias:

- **The Trap:** We feel the pain of losses more acutely than the pleasure of gains. This can lead to holding onto losing positions hoping they'll rebound, or selling winning positions too early to lock in a small profit.
- **Example:** An investor might refuse to sell a stock that's down 20%, hoping it will eventually recover, even if the fundamentals suggest otherwise.

3. Anchoring Bias:

- **The Trap:** We fixate on an initial piece of information (like the price we paid for a stock) and use it as a reference point for all future decisions. This can prevent us from objectively assessing new information and adjusting our strategies accordingly.
- **Example:** A trader might refuse to sell a stock below its purchase price, even if the market conditions have changed significantly.

4. Confirmation Bias:

- **The Trap:** We seek out information that confirms our existing beliefs and ignore evidence that contradicts them. This can lead to tunnel vision and prevent us from seeing the full picture.
- **Example:** An investor who believes a certain stock is a good buy might only read positive news articles about the company, ignoring any negative analysis.

5. Herding Bias:

- **The Trap:** We follow the crowd, even if it means ignoring our own analysis or judgment. This can lead to asset bubbles and crashes as everyone rushes to buy or sell at the same time.
- **Example:** A surge in retail investors buying a particular stock based on social media hype, even if the company's fundamentals are weak.

6. Recency Bias:

- **The Trap:** We give more weight to recent events or information than to older data. This can lead to chasing trends or overreacting to short-term market fluctuations.
- **Example:** An investor might buy a stock that has recently surged in price, assuming the trend will continue, without considering the long-term outlook.

7. Availability Bias:

- **The Trap:** We overestimate the probability of events that are easy to recall or that receive a lot of media attention.
- **Example:** A trader might overestimate the risk of a market crash because they vividly remember the 2008 financial crisis, leading to overly cautious investment decisions.

How to Combat Behavioral Biases:

- **Awareness:** The first step is to recognize that we're all susceptible to biases.
- **Education:** Learn about common biases and their potential impact on your trading decisions.
- **Discipline:** Develop a trading plan with clear rules and stick to it, even when emotions run high.
- **Diversification:** Don't put all your eggs in one basket. Diversify your portfolio to reduce risk.
- **Seek Outside Perspective:** Consult with a financial advisor or mentor who can provide objective advice.

Impact of Sentiment on Market Microstructure

Think of sentiment as the emotional undercurrent that can either calm or roil the waters of the financial market.

How Sentiment Affects Market Microstructure:

1. **Liquidity:**
   - **Positive Sentiment:** When investors are optimistic, they're more likely to trade actively, increasing buying and selling activity. This leads to higher liquidity, making it easier to buy or sell assets without causing large price swings.
   - **Negative Sentiment:** Fear and pessimism can lead to a reluctance to trade, causing liquidity to dry up. This can result in wider bid-ask spreads, higher transaction costs, and increased volatility.

2. **Volatility:**
- **Positive Sentiment:** Optimism often leads to lower volatility, as investors are more confident in the market and less likely to react to short-term fluctuations.
- **Negative Sentiment:** Fear and uncertainty can trigger panic selling and herd behavior, leading to heightened volatility and sharper price movements.

3. **Order Flow:**
- **Positive Sentiment:** Bullish sentiment can lead to a surge of buy orders, creating a bid-side imbalance that pushes prices higher.
- **Negative Sentiment:** Bearish sentiment can trigger a wave of sell orders, causing an ask-side imbalance that drives prices lower.

4. **Price Discovery:**
- **Positive Sentiment:** Optimistic investors may overvalue assets, leading to temporary price bubbles.
- **Negative Sentiment:** Pessimistic investors may undervalue assets, creating opportunities for contrarian investors.

5. **Market Efficiency:**
- **Positive Sentiment:** Optimism can sometimes lead to a "herd mentality," where investors blindly follow the crowd, potentially leading to market inefficiencies.
- **Negative Sentiment:** Fear and panic selling can also lead to irrational behavior and inefficient pricing.

Measuring Sentiment:

Sentiment is difficult to quantify, but there are several ways to gauge it:

- **Market Sentiment Indicators:** These include measures like the VIX (volatility index), put/call ratios, and surveys of investor sentiment.
- **News and Social Media Analysis:** Analyzing news articles, social media posts, and other forms of media can provide insights into the prevailing mood of investors.

Sentiment is a factor that traders and investors need to be aware of, as it can create both opportunities and risks. By understanding how sentiment affects liquidity, volatility, order flow, and price discovery, you can make more informed decisions.

CHAPTER 10: HIGH-FREQUENCY TRADING AND TECHNOLOGY

Evolution of High-Frequency Trading

The story of HFT begins with the broader trend of algorithmic trading (AT). In the 1980s and 90s, computers started to replace human traders, executing orders based on pre-programmed rules. This shift was driven by the rise of electronic trading platforms and the increasing availability of market data.

The Birth of HFT: Decimalization and Reg NMS

Two key developments in the early 2000s accelerated the rise of HFT:

1. **Decimalization:** The move from fractional pricing (e.g., 1/16th of a dollar) to decimal pricing (e.g., $0.01) narrowed bid-ask spreads, creating opportunities for traders to profit from tiny price discrepancies.
2. **Regulation NMS (National Market System):** This regulation required brokers to route orders to the venue with the best price, leading to market fragmentation and creating incentives for firms to develop faster and more sophisticated trading systems.

The Rise of HFT: Speed Becomes King

With the stage set, HFT firms entered the scene, armed with powerful computers, co-located servers near exchanges, and ultra-low latency connections. These firms focused on speed, aiming to execute trades in microseconds to capture fleeting opportunities.

The HFT Landscape Today:

- **Sophisticated Algorithms:** HFT firms employ complex algorithms that analyze vast amounts of data in real-time to identify and exploit fleeting patterns and anomalies.
- **Market Making:** Many HFT firms act as market makers, providing liquidity to the market and earning rebates from exchanges for their services.
- **Arbitrage:** HFT algorithms excel at arbitrage, exploiting tiny price differences between markets or securities.
- **Controversies:** HFT has been criticized for its role in flash crashes and its potential to create an unfair playing field for smaller traders.

The Future of HFT:

The evolution of HFT is far from over. New technologies like machine learning and artificial intelligence are being integrated into HFT strategies, further enhancing their speed and sophistication. The race for speed continues, with firms exploring cutting-edge technologies like quantum computing to gain an even greater edge.

Key Takeaways:

- HFT is a product of technological advancement and regulatory change.
- Speed is the defining characteristic of HFT, with trades executed in microseconds.
- HFT has both benefits (increased liquidity, narrower spreads) and drawbacks (potential for volatility and unfairness).
- The future of HFT is likely to be shaped by new technologies and ongoing regulatory scrutiny.

Impact of Technology on Trading

Let's break down how tech has changed the game:

1. **The Rise of Electronic Trading:**
- **Goodbye, Trading Floors:** Remember those chaotic trading floors with shouting and hand signals? Technology replaced that with electronic exchanges where computers match orders in the blink of an eye.
- **Hello, Accessibility:** Now anyone with an internet connection and a brokerage account can trade. This has democratized access to markets but also increased the number of participants, creating new dynamics.

2. **Algorithmic Trading Takes Over:**
- **Rules-Based Trading:** Computers now execute a huge chunk of trades based on pre-programmed instructions. This has removed human emotion from the equation, but also introduced new risks (think flash crashes).
- **High-Frequency Trading (HFT):** This is algorithmic trading on steroids, where trades happen in microseconds. HFT firms have become major players, providing liquidity but also raising concerns about fairness and market stability.

3. **Data Deluge and Analysis:**
- **Information Overload:** The amount of market data available has exploded. This data deluge has given rise to quantitative trading strategies that rely on crunching numbers to find patterns and predict price movements.

- **Data as an Asset:** High-quality, real-time data has become a valuable commodity in itself, with firms investing heavily in data feeds and analytics tools.

4. **Fragmentation and Interconnectedness:**
- **Multiple Trading Venues:** Exchanges, dark pools, and alternative trading systems (ATS) all compete for order flow. This fragmentation has made markets more complex but also created opportunities for new players.
- **Complex Order Routing:** Brokers use sophisticated algorithms to route orders to the best possible venue, but this can also lead to concerns about conflicts of interest and fairness.

5. **The Rise of Retail Trading:**
- **Mobile Apps and Commission-Free Trading:** User-friendly platforms and the elimination of trading fees have opened the doors to a new generation of retail investors.
- **Social Media and Sentiment:** Platforms like Reddit and Twitter now play a role in market sentiment, sometimes leading to coordinated buying sprees and increased volatility (remember GameStop?).

Technological Challenges and Advancements

This is where the rubber meets the road, where cutting-edge tech can mean the difference between profit and loss in the blink of an eye.

The Need for Speed: The Never-Ending Race

- **Latency is Key:** In the HFT world, speed is everything. Traders are constantly seeking ways to reduce latency – the time it takes for an order to travel from their computer to the exchange and back. Even a few milliseconds can make a huge difference.
- **The Arms Race:** This has led to an arms race in technology, with firms investing heavily in faster hardware, software, and network infrastructure. Co-location (placing servers directly next to exchange servers) has become commonplace.
- **Microwave Networks:** Some firms have even gone as far as using microwave towers to transmit data, as microwaves travel faster than fiber optic cables.

Technological Challenges:

- **Complexity:** HFT systems are incredibly complex, requiring specialized knowledge and expertise to develop and maintain.

- **Cost:** The race for speed is expensive. Investing in the latest technology can be a significant barrier to entry for smaller firms.
- **Regulation:** Regulators are constantly trying to keep up with technological advances, and new rules can impact the profitability and strategies of HFT firms.
- **Cybersecurity:** HFT firms are prime targets for cyberattacks, as even a brief outage can lead to significant losses. Protecting their systems is a constant challenge.

Technological Advancements:

- **Hardware Acceleration:** Firms are using specialized hardware, like field-programmable gate arrays (FPGAs), to speed up calculations and order execution.
- **Artificial Intelligence (AI):** AI and machine learning are being used to analyze vast amounts of data, identify patterns, and make faster trading decisions.
- **Quantum Computing:** This emerging technology has the potential to revolutionize HFT by enabling even faster calculations and analysis.
- **Cloud Computing:** Cloud-based infrastructure can provide scalability and flexibility for HFT firms, allowing them to quickly adapt to changing market conditions.

The Impact on Market Microstructure:

- **Increased Liquidity:** HFT has generally increased liquidity in markets, as it provides a constant stream of orders and narrows bid-ask spreads.
- **Increased Volatility:** The speed and volume of HFT can also contribute to increased volatility, especially during periods of stress.
- **Market Fragmentation:** HFT has played a role in the fragmentation of markets, as firms seek to trade on multiple venues to gain a speed advantage.

Co-location and Proximity Hosting Services

In HFT, where milliseconds matter, being physically close to the exchange's matching engine can be the difference between profit and loss.

What is Co-location?

Co-location is exactly what it sounds like: placing your trading servers in the same physical location as the exchange's matching engine. This means your orders travel the shortest possible distance to be executed, reducing latency (the time it takes for an order to travel to the exchange and back) to the absolute minimum.

Why Co-location Matters in HFT:

- **Speed:** In HFT, speed is #1. Co-location gives firms a significant speed advantage over those whose servers are located farther away.
- **Reduced Slippage:** Slippage is the difference between the expected price of a trade and the actual price. Lower latency means less time for prices to change before your order is executed, reducing slippage.
- **Increased Order Fill Rates:** Being closer to the exchange means your orders are more likely to be filled before others, increasing your chances of profiting from fleeting opportunities.

Proximity Hosting: A Close Cousin

Proximity hosting is a close alternative to co-location. Instead of being directly inside the exchange, servers are housed in data centers located very close to the exchange, often just a few blocks away. This still provides a significant latency advantage over servers located farther away.

Benefits of Co-location and Proximity Hosting:

- **Competitive Edge:** In the ultra-competitive world of HFT, even a small latency advantage can make a big difference.
- **Access to Market Data:** Co-located servers often have direct access to the exchange's data feeds, providing the most up-to-date market information.
- **Improved Risk Management:** Lower latency allows for faster risk checks and order cancellations, reducing the risk of losses due to market fluctuations.

The Cost of Speed:

Co-location and proximity hosting are not cheap. Firms pay a premium for rack space, power, and connectivity. This high cost creates a barrier to entry for smaller firms, leading to concerns about fairness and a potential concentration of market power in the hands of a few well-funded players.

The Regulatory Landscape:

Regulators are keeping a close eye on co-location and proximity hosting, as they can create an uneven playing field. Some exchanges have implemented rules to ensure fair access to these services, such as randomized allocation of rack space or minimum latency requirements for all participants.

Latency Arbitrage Strategies

Latency arbitrage is a high-frequency trading (HFT) strategy that exploits tiny time delays in the dissemination of market information.

What is Latency Arbitrage?

Think of it like this: two exchanges are trading the same stock, but one exchange is slightly slower than the other in updating its prices. A latency arbitrageur, armed with ultra-fast technology and a direct feed of price data, can detect this tiny delay. They buy the stock on the faster exchange at the lower price and simultaneously sell it on the slower exchange at the higher price, pocketing the difference. It's like buying something at a discount in one store and immediately selling it for a profit in another.

How Does it Work?

- **Technology is Key:** Latency arbitrageurs invest heavily in high-speed infrastructure, including co-located servers, specialized hardware, and microwave networks, to minimize the time it takes for their orders to reach the exchange.
- **Data Feeds:** They subscribe to direct data feeds from exchanges, giving them a real-time view of market prices.
- **Algorithms:** Sophisticated algorithms constantly scan for price discrepancies between exchanges and automatically execute trades when a profitable opportunity is detected.

The Benefits and Risks:

- **Benefits:** For the arbitrageur, the benefits are clear: potential for consistent, low-risk profits. For the market, latency arbitrage can theoretically improve price efficiency by quickly eliminating price discrepancies across exchanges.
- **Risks:**
    - **Technological Arms Race:** The constant pursuit of speed can lead to an expensive arms race, with firms investing heavily in ever-faster technology.
    - **Market Manipulation:** Some argue that latency arbitrage can be used for manipulative practices like quote stuffing or spoofing, which can harm market integrity.
    - **Flash Crashes:** HFT strategies, including latency arbitrage, have been implicated in flash crashes, where prices plummet rapidly and then recover.

The Regulatory Landscape:

Latency arbitrage has attracted regulatory scrutiny due to concerns about fairness and market stability. Some regulators have proposed or implemented measures to curb these practices, such as:

- **Minimum Resting Times:** Requiring orders to rest in the order book for a minimum period before they can be canceled, preventing HFT firms from rapidly canceling orders if they don't get immediate execution.
- **Randomization:** Introducing random delays in order processing to level the playing field between HFT firms and other market participants.
- **Monitoring and Surveillance:** Enhancing market surveillance to detect and deter manipulative practices.

CHAPTER 11: REGULATION AND MARKET MICROSTRUCTURE

Key Regulatory Bodies and Their Roles

The regulatory bodies that oversee market microstructure set the rules of the game, ensuring fair play, protecting investors, and maintaining the overall integrity of the markets.

Key Regulatory Bodies and Their Roles:

1. Securities and Exchange Commission (SEC) - United States:

- **Oversight:** Regulates securities markets, including exchanges, broker-dealers, and investment advisors.
- **Mandate:** Protects investors, maintains fair and orderly markets, and facilitates capital formation.
- **Market Microstructure Focus:** Sets rules for market structure, trading practices, and disclosure requirements. Monitors market activity for potential manipulation and fraud.

2. Financial Industry Regulatory Authority (FINRA) - United States:

- **Oversight:** Oversees broker-dealers and enforces rules related to trading practices and sales practices.
- **Mandate:** Protects investors and ensures market integrity.
- **Market Microstructure Focus:** Conducts market surveillance, investigates potential violations, and educates investors about market risks.

3. Commodity Futures Trading Commission (CFTC) - United States:

- **Oversight:** Regulates derivatives markets, including futures and options on commodities and financial instruments.
- **Mandate:** Protects market participants from fraud, manipulation, and abusive practices.
- **Market Microstructure Focus:** Sets rules for margin requirements, position limits, and trading practices in derivatives markets.

4. European Securities and Markets Authority (ESMA) - European Union:

- **Oversight:** Coordinates securities regulation across the EU, including market structure and transparency.
- **Mandate:** Protects investors, ensures market integrity, and promotes financial stability.
- **Market Microstructure Focus:** Develops and implements rules for MiFID II, a major regulation that governs investment services and trading venues in the EU.

5. Financial Conduct Authority (FCA) - United Kingdom:

- **Oversight:** Regulates financial markets and firms in the UK, including market conduct and consumer protection.
- **Mandate:** Protects consumers, ensures market integrity, and promotes competition.
- **Market Microstructure Focus:** Oversees trading venues, market makers, and HFT firms, enforcing rules related to market abuse and best execution.

Other Key Regulators:

- **Monetary Authority of Singapore (MAS):** Regulates financial markets in Singapore.
- **Securities and Futures Commission (SFC) - Hong Kong:** Oversees securities and futures markets in Hong Kong.
- **Japan Financial Services Agency (FSA):** Regulates financial markets in Japan.

The Importance of Regulation:

- **Investor Protection:** Regulations are designed to protect investors from fraud, manipulation, and unfair practices.
- **Market Integrity:** Regulations ensure that markets are fair, transparent, and orderly, promoting investor confidence.
- **Financial Stability:** Regulations aim to mitigate systemic risk and prevent market disruptions that could harm the broader economy.

The Challenge of Keeping Up:

Market microstructure is constantly evolving, with new technologies and trading practices emerging all the time. Regulators face the challenge of keeping up with these changes and adapting regulations to ensure they remain effective in protecting investors and maintaining market integrity.

Major Regulatory Frameworks

These frameworks are like the rulebooks for financial markets, designed to ensure fairness, transparency, and stability while helping with competition and innovation.

1. Regulation NMS (National Market System) - United States:

- **Purpose:** Aims to create a fair and efficient national market system for equities in the U.S.
- **Key Provisions:**
    - **Order Protection Rule:** Requires brokers to route orders to the venue with the best price, promoting price competition among exchanges.
    - **Trade-Through Rule:** Prohibits trades that occur at prices inferior to those displayed on other exchanges.
    - **Market Access Rule:** Requires fair and non-discriminatory access to quotes and trading.
- **Impact on Market Microstructure:** Increased market fragmentation, led to the rise of alternative trading systems (ATS) and dark pools, and intensified competition among trading venues.

2. Dodd-Frank Wall Street Reform and Consumer Protection Act - United States:

- **Purpose:** Aims to prevent another financial crisis by increasing oversight and regulation of financial institutions.
- **Key Provisions:**
    - **Volcker Rule:** Restricts proprietary trading by banks (trading for their own profit).
    - **Regulation of Derivatives:** Mandates central clearing and exchange trading for standardized derivatives.
    - **Enhanced Consumer Protection:** Creates the Consumer Financial Protection Bureau (CFPB) to protect consumers from abusive financial practices.
- **Impact on Market Microstructure:** Reduced risk-taking by banks, increased transparency in derivatives markets, and greater focus on consumer protection.

3. Markets in Financial Instruments Directive (MiFID II) - European Union:

- **Purpose:** Harmonizes financial markets regulation across the EU, promoting transparency, competition, and investor protection.
- **Key Provisions:**
    - **Best Execution:** Requires firms to take all sufficient steps to obtain the best possible result for their clients when executing orders.
    - **Transparency:** Mandates pre- and post-trade transparency for a wider range of financial instruments.

- - **Product Governance:** Imposes stricter rules on product design and distribution to ensure suitability for investors.
  - **Algorithmic and High-Frequency Trading:** Introduces stricter rules for algorithmic and high-frequency trading, including requirements for risk controls and testing.
- **Impact on Market Microstructure:** Increased transparency, greater competition among trading venues, and stricter oversight of algorithmic trading.

4. Markets in Financial Instruments Regulation (MiFIR) - European Union:

- **Purpose:** Complements MiFID II by setting out the technical rules for trading and reporting.
- **Key Provisions:**
  - **Trade Reporting:** Mandates reporting of all trades to approved reporting mechanisms.
  - **Transaction Reporting:** Requires firms to report details of transactions to regulators.
  - **Transparency Requirements:** Sets out rules for the publication of pre- and post-trade data.
- **Impact on Market Microstructure:** Enhanced market transparency and improved data quality for regulators and market participants.

5. Other Key Regulations:

- **Regulation SHO - United States:** Governs short selling in the U.S.
- **Market Abuse Regulation (MAR) - European Union:** Prohibits insider trading and market manipulation.
- **Volatility Regulation:** Various regulations, like circuit breakers and volatility auctions, aim to curb excessive volatility in markets.

Impact of Regulation on Market Behavior

Regulations can change the way people trade, the tools they use, and even the prices we see in the market.

How Regulation Shapes Market Behavior:

1. **Tick Sizes and Price Increments:**
   - **The Rule:** Regulations often set minimum price increments (tick sizes) at which securities can be quoted or traded. This is designed to prevent excessive price volatility and ensure orderly markets.

- **The Impact:** Smaller tick sizes can lead to narrower bid-ask spreads, reducing trading costs for investors. However, they can also make it harder for market makers to profit, potentially reducing liquidity. Larger tick sizes can have the opposite effect.

2. **Order Types and Trading Practices:**
- **The Rule:** Regulators can restrict or even ban certain order types, such as "spoofing" (placing orders with no intention of executing them) or "layering" (placing multiple orders to create a false impression of market depth). They may also impose rules on how quickly orders can be cancelled or modified.
- **The Impact:** These rules aim to prevent manipulative practices and promote fair markets. However, they can also limit trading strategies and impact market liquidity.

3. **Transparency and Disclosure:**
- **The Rule:** Regulations often require pre-trade and post-trade transparency, meaning that information about orders and trades must be made public. This can include order book data, trade prices, and volumes.
- **The Impact:** Transparency can improve price discovery, reduce information asymmetry, and deter market manipulation. However, it can also discourage large traders from participating, as they don't want to reveal their intentions.

4. **High-Frequency Trading (HFT):**
- **The Rule:** Regulators are increasingly scrutinizing HFT due to concerns about its impact on market stability and fairness. Some have implemented rules to slow down HFT, such as minimum resting times for orders or "speed bumps" that introduce random delays.
- **The Impact:** These regulations aim to level the playing field between HFT firms and other market participants. However, they can also reduce liquidity and increase trading costs.

5. **Market Access and Competition:**
- **The Rule:** Regulators aim to promote competition among trading venues by ensuring fair and non-discriminatory access to markets. This can involve rules on order routing, co-location, and market data fees.
- **The Impact:** Competition can lead to lower trading costs, increased innovation, and improved market quality. However, it can also lead to market fragmentation, making it harder to track prices and understand overall market dynamics.

6. **Circuit Breakers and Volatility Controls:**

- **The Rule:** Circuit breakers are temporary halts in trading that are triggered when prices move too far or too fast. Volatility auctions are designed to find a fair price after a trading halt.
- **The Impact:** These mechanisms aim to prevent panic selling and extreme market volatility. However, they can also disrupt trading and create uncertainty.

The Unintended Consequences:

While regulations are designed with good intentions, they can sometimes have unintended consequences. For example, regulations aimed at reducing risk-taking by banks may lead them to withdraw from market making activities, reducing liquidity.

Regulatory Challenges and Responses

The Challenges:

1. **The Speed of Technology:**
- **High-frequency trading (HFT)**: The lightning-fast pace of HFT poses challenges for regulators in terms of monitoring, surveillance, and ensuring fair access to markets.
- **Algorithmic trading**: The complexity and opacity of algorithms make it difficult for regulators to detect potential market manipulation or unintended consequences.
- **Cybersecurity threats**: The increasing reliance on technology exposes markets to cyber attacks, raising concerns about market integrity and investor protection.

2. **Market Fragmentation:**
- **Proliferation of trading venues**: The rise of alternative trading systems (ATS) and dark pools has fragmented liquidity, making it harder to track prices and understand market dynamics.
- **Regulatory arbitrage**: Traders may exploit differences in regulations across different venues, creating an uneven playing field.

3. **Complex Products and Practices:**
- **Derivatives**: The complexity of derivatives markets poses challenges for risk management and transparency.
- **High-frequency market making**: While providing liquidity, HFT market makers can also engage in practices like quote stuffing and spoofing, which can disrupt markets and harm other participants.

4. **Cross-Border Issues:**

- **Regulatory differences**: Varying regulations across jurisdictions can create opportunities for regulatory arbitrage and make it difficult to enforce consistent standards.
- **Cross-border trading**: The global nature of financial markets makes it challenging to monitor and regulate cross-border trading activity.

Regulatory Responses:

Regulators have responded to these challenges with a range of measures, including:

1. **Increased Transparency:**
- **Pre- and post-trade transparency**: Regulations like MiFID II in Europe require greater transparency of trading activity, including the publication of pre- and post-trade data.
- **Trade reporting**: Mandatory trade reporting helps regulators monitor market activity and detect potential manipulation.
- **Increased disclosure requirements for HFT firms**: This helps to shed light on their activities and mitigate potential risks.

2. **Circuit Breakers and Volatility Controls:**
- **Circuit breakers**: Temporary trading halts are triggered when prices move too far or too fast to prevent panic selling and market instability.
- **Volatility auctions**: These mechanisms help to find a fair price after a trading halt and restore orderly trading.

3. **Regulation of HFT and Algorithmic Trading:**
- **Registration and supervision**: HFT firms are subject to stricter registration and supervision requirements to ensure they have adequate risk controls and operate in a fair and orderly manner.
- **Restrictions on certain practices**: Regulators have banned or restricted practices like spoofing and layering, which are considered manipulative.
- **Speed bumps and minimum resting times**: Some regulators have implemented measures to slow down HFT and level the playing field with other market participants.

4. **Market Surveillance and Enforcement:**
- **Enhanced surveillance**: Regulators are investing in technology and data analytics to monitor market activity in real-time and detect potential market abuse.
- **Stronger enforcement**: Penalties for market manipulation and other violations have been increased to deter bad actors.
- **International cooperation**: Regulators are increasingly cooperating with each other across borders to tackle cross-border regulatory arbitrage and ensure consistent enforcement.

The Ongoing Challenge:

The regulatory landscape is constantly evolving, and regulators must remain vigilant and adaptable. New technologies and trading practices will continue to emerge, requiring ongoing review and adjustment of regulations. The goal is to strike the right balance between protecting investors, maintaining market integrity, and fostering innovation in financial markets.

CHAPTER 12: MARKET CRISES AND MICROSTRUCTURE

Historical Market Crises and Their Causes

Let's look into some pivotal moments in financial history – market crises where microstructure played a significant role, either as a contributing factor or by revealing vulnerabilities in the system.

1987 Black Monday:

- **The Crisis:** On October 19, 1987, the Dow Jones Industrial Average plummeted 22.6% in a single day, the largest one-day percentage drop in history.
- **Microstructure Role:** Several factors contributed to the crash, but the prevalent use of program trading (a precursor to algorithmic trading) was a major culprit. These programs, designed to automatically execute trades based on pre-set triggers, created a cascade of selling that exacerbated the decline.
- **Key Takeaway:** This crisis highlighted the risks of automated trading and the potential for market instability when liquidity dries up.

1998 Long-Term Capital Management (LTCM) Collapse:

- **The Crisis:** LTCM, a highly leveraged hedge fund, faced massive losses due to the Russian financial crisis and a flight to quality. Its near-collapse threatened to destabilize global markets.
- **Microstructure Role:** LTCM's complex trading strategies relied on highly liquid markets to function. When liquidity dried up, they were unable to unwind their positions, leading to a downward spiral.
- **Key Takeaway:** This crisis underscored the importance of liquidity risk management and the dangers of excessive leverage, especially in illiquid markets.

2010 Flash Crash:

- **The Crisis:** On May 6, 2010, the Dow Jones Industrial Average plunged almost 1,000 points in minutes before quickly recovering.
- **Microstructure Role:** The crash was triggered by a large sell order executed by a mutual fund using an algorithmic trading strategy. The algorithm's aggressive selling behavior, coupled with thin liquidity and a fragmented market structure, amplified the price decline.

- **Key Takeaway:** This event highlighted the potential risks of algorithmic trading and the need for robust risk controls to prevent unintended market disruptions.

2021 GameStop Short Squeeze:

- **The Crisis:** Retail investors, coordinating on social media, drove up the price of GameStop stock, causing massive losses for hedge funds that had bet against the company.
- **Microstructure Role:** The unusual trading activity triggered margin calls for short sellers, forcing them to buy back shares to cover their positions. This buying pressure further fueled the price surge, creating a classic short squeeze.
- **Key Takeaway:** This episode demonstrated the power of social media to influence market sentiment and the potential risks of concentrated short positions in a highly interconnected market.

Other Notable Crises:

- **1997 Asian Financial Crisis:** Contagion effects and a lack of transparency in some markets exacerbated the crisis.
- **2008 Financial Crisis:** The collapse of the housing bubble exposed weaknesses in the mortgage-backed securities market and triggered a global financial crisis.

Key Lessons Learned:

- **Liquidity Matters:** Liquidity is essential for market stability. When liquidity dries up, even small shocks can trigger large price movements.
- **Technology is a Double-Edged Sword:** While technology has made markets more efficient, it has also introduced new risks, like the potential for flash crashes and algorithmic trading errors.
- **Regulation Plays a Key Role:** Robust regulation is needed to ensure market integrity, prevent manipulation, and protect investors.
- **Understanding Microstructure is Crucial:** Analyzing market crises through the lens of microstructure helps us understand how different market participants, trading strategies, and regulations interact to shape market outcomes.

By studying historical market crises, we can learn valuable lessons about the strengths and weaknesses of market microstructure and develop better strategies for managing risk and promoting stability in the future.

Role of Market Microstructure in Crises

Let's examine how market microstructure, the nuts and bolts of how trading happens, can either contribute to or expose vulnerabilities during financial crises.

Market Microstructure as a Contributing Factor:

1. **Liquidity Evaporation:**
   - **The Issue:** In a crisis, fear and uncertainty often lead to a rapid withdrawal of liquidity. Market makers may step back, and investors may hoard cash, making it difficult to buy or sell assets at reasonable prices.
   - **Microstructure Role:** Market structures with limited participation or reliance on a few key players can be particularly vulnerable to liquidity droughts. Fragmented markets can also experience uneven liquidity across different venues, exacerbating price swings.

2. **Contagion and Feedback Loops:**
   - **The Issue:** Crises can spread rapidly across markets and asset classes as panicked investors sell off assets to cover losses or meet margin calls.
   - **Microstructure Role:** Interconnectedness between markets, facilitated by high-speed trading and algorithmic strategies, can accelerate this contagion effect. Feedback loops, where falling prices trigger more selling, can amplify the downward spiral.

3. **Information Asymmetry and Panic:**
   - **The Issue:** During crises, information can become scarce or unreliable, leading to uncertainty and fear. This can trigger panic selling as investors try to get out before it's too late.
   - **Microstructure Role:** Opaque markets, such as dark pools, where trading information is hidden, can exacerbate information asymmetry and contribute to panic.

4. **Operational and Technical Risks:**
   - **The Issue:** Crises can expose weaknesses in clearing and settlement systems, trading platforms, and risk management models. Technical glitches or failures can disrupt trading and amplify market stress.
   - **Microstructure Role:** Complex market structures with multiple trading venues and intricate trading algorithms can be vulnerable to operational risks, especially during periods of high volume and volatility.

Market Microstructure as a Diagnostic Tool:

While market microstructure can contribute to crises, it also provides valuable tools for understanding and responding to them:

1. **Identifying Vulnerabilities:** Analyzing trading patterns, order flow, and liquidity dynamics during a crisis can reveal weaknesses in market structure and identify areas for improvement.
2. **Early Warning Signals:** Monitoring market microstructure data can help detect early warning signs of a brewing crisis, such as declining liquidity, increasing volatility, or unusual trading activity.
3. **Stress Testing:** Simulating crisis scenarios using market microstructure models can help assess the resilience of markets and identify potential vulnerabilities before they become critical.
4. **Regulatory Response:** Insights from market microstructure research can inform regulatory responses to crises, helping policymakers design rules that promote stability and resilience.

Lessons Learned and Preventive Measures

Each crisis, while painful, has offered insights that we can apply to strengthen our financial systems.

1. The Critical Importance of Liquidity:

- **The Lesson:** Liquidity is the lifeblood of markets. When it dries up, even small shocks can trigger a cascade of selling and dramatic price drops. We saw this vividly in the 1987 Black Monday crash and the 2008 financial crisis.
- **Preventive Measures:**
    - **Robust Market Making:** Encourage and incentivize market makers to provide liquidity, even during stressed conditions. This can involve offering rebates, reducing regulatory burdens, or exploring new models like auction mechanisms during volatility spikes.
    - **Central Bank Intervention:** Central banks can act as lenders of last resort, providing liquidity to markets when it dries up.
    - **Pre-Funding Requirements:** Require financial institutions to hold sufficient liquid assets to meet potential obligations during market stress.

2. The Double-Edged Sword of Technology:

- **The Lesson:** Technology has revolutionized trading, but it can also introduce new risks. Algorithmic trading and high-frequency trading (HFT), while increasing efficiency, can amplify volatility and contribute to flash crashes (as seen in the 2010 Flash Crash).
- **Preventive Measures:**

- **Robust Risk Controls:** Require firms to have rigorous risk management systems in place to prevent rogue algorithms and unintended consequences.
- **Circuit Breakers:** Implement circuit breakers that pause trading during periods of extreme volatility, giving markets time to cool down and preventing cascading sell-offs.
- **Monitoring and Surveillance:** Invest in sophisticated surveillance technology to detect and deter manipulative trading practices.

3. The Perils of Interconnectedness:

- **The Lesson:** While interconnectedness can improve price discovery and efficiency, it can also accelerate the spread of crises across markets. We witnessed this in the 1997 Asian financial crisis and the 2008 global financial crisis.
- **Preventive Measures:**
    - **Stress Testing:** Regularly test the resilience of interconnected markets under various stress scenarios to identify vulnerabilities.
    - **Capital Buffers:** Require financial institutions to hold additional capital buffers to absorb losses and prevent contagion.
    - **Coordination among Regulators:** Foster international cooperation among regulators to monitor cross-border risks and coordinate responses to global crises.

4. The Power of Information (and Disinformation):

- **The Lesson:** Information (or the lack of it) can significantly impact market sentiment and behavior. Rumors and misinformation can quickly trigger panic selling, as seen in the 2021 GameStop short squeeze.
- **Preventive Measures:**
    - **Transparency and Disclosure:** Require greater transparency from market participants, including hedge funds and institutional investors, to reduce information asymmetry.
    - **Real-Time Market Data:** Make high-quality market data readily available to all participants, including retail investors, to level the playing field.
    - **Combating Fake News:** Implement measures to detect and counter the spread of false or misleading information.

5. The Human Element:

- **The Lesson:** Behavioral biases, like herding and overconfidence, can amplify market volatility and exacerbate crises.
- **Preventive Measures:**
    - **Investor Education:** Educate investors about behavioral biases and encourage them to develop disciplined trading strategies.

- **Cooling-Off Periods:** Introduce mandatory waiting periods for certain types of trades, giving investors time to reconsider impulsive decisions.

Market crises are inevitable, but we can learn from history and take steps to mitigate their impact. By understanding the role of market microstructure, we can design more resilient markets, improve risk management, and ultimately protect investors and the broader economy.

CHAPTER 13: QUANTITATIVE METHODS IN MARKET MICROSTRUCTURE

Statistical Tools and Models

Statistical tools and models are essential for dissecting market microstructure. They help us quantify and analyze the vast amounts of data generated by trading activity, uncovering hidden patterns, testing theories, and ultimately gaining a deeper understanding of how markets function.

Key Statistical Tools:

1. **Descriptive Statistics:**
- **Purpose:** Summarize and describe key features of market data, such as:
    - Central tendency (mean, median, mode): What's the average price or trade size?
    - Dispersion (variance, standard deviation): How spread out are the prices or trade sizes?
    - Skewness and kurtosis: Are the distributions of prices or returns symmetrical or skewed? Are the tails fat or thin?

2. **Regression Analysis:**
- **Purpose:** Model the relationship between different variables, such as:
    - Price and trading volume: How does volume affect price changes?
    - Volatility and trading activity: Is volatility related to the number of trades?
    - Bid-ask spread and market depth: How does the spread change with market depth?

3. **Time Series Analysis:**
- **Purpose:** Analyze how market variables change over time, including:
    - Autocorrelation: Do past prices predict future prices?
    - Stationarity: Do the statistical properties of a time series remain constant over time?
    - Volatility Clustering: Do periods of high volatility tend to cluster together?

4. **Event Study Analysis:**
- **Purpose:** Examine the impact of specific events (like earnings announcements or news releases) on asset prices.

- **Methodology:** Compare the actual price movement after the event to what would have been expected based on normal market conditions.

Key Statistical Models:

1. **Roll Model:**
- **Purpose:** Estimate the effective bid-ask spread using the serial covariance of price changes.
- **Assumption:** The bid-ask spread is the primary cause of negative serial covariance in price changes.

2. **Amihud-Mendelson Model:**
- **Purpose:** Analyze the relationship between liquidity (measured by trading volume or bid-ask spread) and asset returns.
- **Assumption:** Illiquid assets require a higher expected return to compensate investors for the higher trading costs associated with illiquidity.

3. **Hasbrouck Model:**
- **Purpose:** Decompose price changes into components related to information and liquidity effects.
- **Assumption:** Information and liquidity are the two main drivers of price changes in the market.

4. **Vector Autoregression (VAR) Models:**
- **Purpose:** Model the dynamic relationships between multiple market variables, such as prices, trading volume, and volatility.
- **Assumption:** The variables in the model are interrelated and influence each other over time.

5. **Agent-Based Models:**
- **Purpose:** Simulate the behavior of individual traders and their interactions to understand how market dynamics emerge.
- **Assumption:** Market behavior can be explained by the actions and interactions of individual agents.

The Importance of Statistical Analysis:

- **Testing Hypotheses:** Statistical tools allow us to test theories about market behavior and assess their validity.
- **Identifying Patterns:** We can uncover hidden patterns and relationships in market data that may not be immediately obvious.
- **Measuring Market Quality:** We can quantify liquidity, price efficiency, and other aspects of market quality using statistical measures.

- **Developing Trading Strategies:** Statistical models can inform the development of algorithmic trading strategies and risk management models.
- **Informing Regulatory Policy:** Statistical analysis can help regulators assess the impact of different market structures and regulations on market outcomes.

Predictive Analytics and Market Trends

Predictive analytics uses statistical models, machine learning algorithms, and data mining techniques to analyze historical and real-time market data. Its goal? To uncover patterns, correlations, and anomalies that can be used to forecast future market trends.

How Does Predictive Analytics Work in Market Microstructure?

1. **Data Collection and Preprocessing:**
- **Vast Datasets:** Predictive analytics requires massive amounts of data, including historical prices, trading volumes, order book data, news sentiment, and even social media chatter.
- **Data Cleaning:** This raw data is cleaned and standardized to ensure accuracy and consistency.
- **Feature Engineering:** Relevant features are extracted from the data, such as technical indicators, order flow imbalances, or sentiment scores.

2. **Model Development:**
- **Machine Learning Algorithms:** Sophisticated algorithms like random forests, neural networks, or support vector machines are trained on historical data to identify patterns and relationships.
- **Model Selection and Validation:** The best-performing model is selected and tested on out-of-sample data to ensure its predictive accuracy.

3. **Real-Time Analysis:**
- **Streaming Data:** The model is fed with real-time market data to generate predictions about future price movements, liquidity conditions, or other market trends.
- **Adaptive Learning:** The model continuously updates itself as new data arrives, adapting to changing market conditions.

Applications of Predictive Analytics in Market Microstructure:

- **Price Prediction:** Forecast short-term price movements based on patterns in historical data, order flow, and news sentiment.

- **Volatility Forecasting:** Predict future volatility levels based on historical patterns, news events, and market sentiment.
- **Liquidity Prediction:** Estimate future liquidity conditions based on order book data, trading volume, and market maker behavior.
- **Trade Execution Optimization:** Use predictive models to determine optimal order placement, timing, and sizing to minimize market impact and transaction costs.
- **Risk Management:** Identify potential risks and vulnerabilities in portfolios or trading strategies based on historical data and market trends.

Challenges and Limitations:

- **Overfitting:** Models may become too specialized in the data they were trained on and fail to generalize to new data.
- **Data Quality:** Accurate and reliable data is crucial for effective predictive analytics. Poor data quality can lead to inaccurate predictions.
- **Model Complexity:** Complex models may be difficult to interpret and explain, making it hard to understand the underlying reasons for their predictions.
- **Changing Market Dynamics:** Market conditions are constantly evolving, making it challenging to develop models that remain accurate over time.

The Future of Predictive Analytics in Market Microstructure:

Predictive analytics is rapidly advancing, with new algorithms and techniques emerging all the time. Some exciting developments on the horizon include:

- **Explainable AI (XAI):** Developing models that can explain their reasoning and decision-making processes, increasing transparency and trust.
- **Alternative Data:** Incorporating a wider range of data sources, such as social media sentiment or satellite imagery, to gain new insights.
- **Real-Time Risk Management:** Developing systems that can dynamically adjust risk management strategies based on real-time market conditions and predictions.

Applications of Machine Learning

Machine learning (ML) has become a game-changer in market microstructure, offering ways to analyze vast amounts of data, uncover hidden patterns, and make predictions with increasing accuracy. Let's explore some of the most impactful applications of ML in this field:

1. High-Frequency Trading (HFT) Strategies:

- **Order Book Prediction:** ML models can analyze real-time order book data, including bid/ask prices, volumes, and order flow, to predict short-term price movements. This allows HFT firms to make rapid trading decisions and potentially profit from fleeting opportunities.
- **Execution Algorithms:** ML algorithms can optimize order execution by dynamically adjusting trading strategies based on market conditions, minimizing market impact, and achieving better prices.

2. Price Prediction and Forecasting:

- **Time Series Analysis:** ML models like recurrent neural networks (RNNs) and long short-term memory (LSTM) networks can analyze historical price data to identify patterns and trends, improving the accuracy of price forecasts.
- **Sentiment Analysis:** ML algorithms can analyze news articles, social media posts, and other sources of textual data to gauge market sentiment and predict its impact on prices.
- **Volatility Prediction:** ML models can forecast future volatility levels based on historical patterns, news events, and market microstructure data.

3. Risk Management and Anomaly Detection:

- **Risk Modeling:** ML algorithms can build sophisticated risk models that take into account a wide range of factors, including market volatility, liquidity, and correlations between assets.
- **Anomaly Detection:** ML can help identify unusual trading patterns or market behavior that may indicate potential risks or opportunities, such as market manipulation or flash crashes.

4. Market Surveillance and Regulatory Compliance:

- **Fraud Detection:** ML algorithms can sift through massive amounts of trading data to detect suspicious activity that may indicate insider trading, market manipulation, or other fraudulent behavior.
- **Compliance Monitoring:** ML can automate the monitoring of trading activities to ensure compliance with regulatory requirements, saving time and resources for both firms and regulators.

5. Liquidity Provision and Market Making:

- **Smart Order Routing:** ML algorithms can optimize order routing by analyzing liquidity across different trading venues and selecting the best execution path.

- **Adaptive Market Making:** ML models can dynamically adjust bid and ask quotes based on real-time market conditions, optimizing market maker profitability while providing liquidity.

6. **Trading Strategy Development and Backtesting:**

- **Strategy Optimization:** ML algorithms can be used to optimize trading strategies by testing them on historical data and identifying parameters that maximize performance.
- **Backtesting:** ML can automate the backtesting process, allowing traders to quickly evaluate the historical performance of different strategies and make data-driven decisions.

7. **Sentiment Analysis and News Analytics:**

- **News Impact Analysis:** ML algorithms can analyze the impact of news events on market prices and sentiment, providing valuable insights for traders and investors.
- **Social Media Monitoring:** ML can track social media conversations to gauge market sentiment and identify potential trends or risks.

Challenges and Considerations:

- **Data Quality and Bias:** ML models heavily rely on data, and if the data is biased or incomplete, the model's predictions can be inaccurate.
- **Interpretability:** Some ML models, like deep neural networks, can be "black boxes," making it difficult to understand the reasoning behind their predictions.
- **Overfitting:** Models can become too specialized in the data they were trained on and fail to generalize to new data, leading to poor out-of-sample performance.

The Future of ML in Market Microstructure:

Machine learning is revolutionizing the field of market microstructure. As technology advances, we can expect even more sophisticated and powerful applications of ML, further enhancing our understanding of market dynamics and improving trading and investment strategies.

Agent-Based Modeling and Simulation

Imagine it as a virtual laboratory where we create a miniature version of a financial market, complete with simulated traders, order books, and all the complex interactions that drive prices and liquidity.

What is Agent-Based Modeling?

ABM is a computational approach to studying complex systems. In the context of market microstructure, it involves creating a virtual market populated by "agents," which are essentially software programs that mimic the behavior of real-world traders. These agents can have different trading strategies, risk preferences, and information sets. We then let them interact with each other and observe how their collective actions shape market outcomes.

Why Use Agent-Based Modeling?

1. **Complexity:** Financial markets are complex systems with many interacting components. Traditional models often struggle to capture this complexity, but ABM can simulate the behavior of individual agents and their interactions, leading to more realistic and nuanced insights.
2. **Flexibility:** ABM allows researchers to experiment with different market structures, trading rules, and agent behaviors to see how they impact market outcomes. This can help us understand the potential consequences of proposed regulatory changes or new trading technologies.
3. **Experimentation:** We can conduct "what-if" scenarios in a simulated environment, testing the impact of various factors on market dynamics without risking real money or disrupting real markets.
4. **Uncovering Emergent Properties:** ABM can reveal emergent properties – unexpected patterns or behaviors that arise from the interactions of individual agents. This can help us understand phenomena like market crashes or liquidity crises that are difficult to explain with traditional models.

How Does Agent-Based Modeling Work?

1. **Agent Design:** We create agents with different characteristics, such as:
    - Trading strategies (e.g., value investors, momentum traders, market makers)
    - Risk preferences (e.g., risk-averse, risk-neutral, risk-seeking)
    - Information sets (e.g., informed vs. uninformed traders)
2. **Market Environment:** We set up a virtual market with an order book, matching engine, and trading rules.
3. **Simulation:** We let the agents interact in the market, placing orders, executing trades, and updating their strategies based on market feedback.
4. **Data Collection:** We collect data on prices, trading volume, order flow, and other market variables.

5. **Analysis:** We analyze the data to identify patterns, test hypotheses, and evaluate the impact of different factors on market outcomes.

Applications of Agent-Based Modeling:

- **Testing Market Designs:** Simulate the impact of different market structures, such as continuous trading vs. auctions, to determine which design promotes the most efficient and stable markets.
- **Evaluating Regulatory Changes:** Test the potential consequences of proposed regulatory changes, such as tick size restrictions or transaction taxes, before they are implemented.
- **Understanding Market Anomalies:** Investigate the causes of market anomalies, such as the January effect or the momentum effect, by simulating the behavior of agents with different biases and strategies.
- **Developing Trading Strategies:** Use ABM to test the effectiveness of different trading strategies and identify optimal parameters.

Challenges and Limitations:

- **Model Validation:** Ensuring that the model accurately reflects real-world market dynamics is crucial. This requires careful calibration and validation against empirical data.
- **Complexity:** ABM models can be computationally intensive, requiring significant computing power and expertise to develop and run.
- **Assumptions:** The results of ABM simulations depend on the assumptions made about agent behavior and market conditions. It's important to be aware of these assumptions and their potential limitations.

Natural Language Processing for News Analytics

Imagine having a tireless research assistant who can read and interpret thousands of news articles, tweets, and financial reports in a matter of seconds, extracting valuable insights that can inform your trading decisions. That's the power of NLP.

What is Natural Language Processing (NLP)?

NLP is a field of artificial intelligence (AI) that focuses on enabling computers to understand, interpret, and generate human language. In the context of market microstructure, NLP algorithms can be used to analyze vast amounts of textual data from news articles, social media posts, financial reports, and other sources to extract information that is relevant to financial markets.

How Does NLP Work in News Analytics?

1. Data Collection:
    - **Diverse Sources:** Gather data from various news outlets, blogs, forums, social media platforms, and regulatory filings.
    - **Real-Time Feeds:** Utilize APIs and web scraping tools to collect news data in real time, ensuring access to the latest information.

2. Text Preprocessing:
    - **Cleaning and Normalization:** Remove noise, correct spelling errors, and standardize text formats to ensure consistency.
    - **Tokenization:** Break down text into smaller units, such as words or phrases, for further analysis.
    - **Stop Word Removal:** Eliminate common words (like "the," "and," "is") that don't carry much meaning.

3. Feature Extraction:
    - **Sentiment Analysis:** Determine the emotional tone of the text (positive, negative, neutral) to gauge market sentiment.
    - **Named Entity Recognition (NER):** Identify and classify key entities in the text, such as companies, people, or financial instruments.
    - **Topic Modeling:** Group similar news articles or social media posts into topics to understand the main themes of the discussion.
    - **Event Extraction:** Identify specific events mentioned in the text, such as earnings announcements, mergers, or regulatory actions.

4. Analysis and Prediction:
    - **Impact Analysis:** Assess the potential impact of news events on specific stocks or the broader market.
    - **Event-Driven Trading:** Develop trading strategies based on the expected impact of news events.
    - **Sentiment-Based Trading:** Trade based on the overall sentiment expressed in news and social media.
    - **Trend Analysis:** Identify emerging trends in news and social media to anticipate market movements.

Applications of NLP in Market Microstructure:

- **Real-Time News Monitoring:** Track news and social media in real time to quickly identify market-moving events and react to them.
- **Sentiment Analysis for Trading:** Gauge market sentiment and use it as an input for trading decisions.
- **Event Detection and Analysis:** Identify and analyze specific events that can impact stock prices or market volatility.

- **News-Based Trading Strategies:** Develop algorithmic trading strategies that automatically execute trades based on news sentiment or specific events.
- **Risk Management:** Monitor news and social media for potential risks that could impact portfolios or trading strategies.

Challenges and Limitations:

- **Ambiguity and Context:** Human language is inherently ambiguous, and understanding the context of news articles or social media posts can be challenging for machines.
- **Data Quality:** News data can be noisy, containing errors, biases, or irrelevant information.
- **Model Accuracy:** NLP models are not perfect and can sometimes misinterpret the meaning of text or make incorrect predictions.

The Future of NLP in Market Microstructure:

NLP is rapidly evolving, with new models and techniques being developed constantly. We can expect to see continued advancements in the ability of machines to understand and interpret human language, leading to more sophisticated and accurate news analytics tools for traders and investors.

CHAPTER 14: FUTURE TRENDS IN MARKET MICROSTRUCTURE

Emerging Technologies and Their Impact

1. **Artificial Intelligence (AI) and Machine Learning (ML): The Brains of the Operation**
- **Predictive Analytics:** AI and ML algorithms are becoming masters at analyzing vast amounts of data to forecast market trends, price movements, and even pinpoint potential risks. They're like the Sherlock Holmes of the trading world, spotting subtle clues that humans might miss.
- **Algorithmic Trading Evolution:** Forget basic rule-based algorithms. We're moving towards more sophisticated AI-powered strategies that can adapt and learn in real-time, constantly refining their approach to market conditions.
- **Sentiment Analysis:** AI can now sift through news articles, social media, and other textual data to gauge market sentiment, giving traders an edge in understanding the emotional drivers of prices.

2. **Blockchain and Distributed Ledger Technology (DLT): The Trust Revolution**
- **Decentralized Exchanges (DEXs):** These peer-to-peer trading platforms eliminate intermediaries, promising greater transparency, security, and reduced costs. They could democratize access to markets and challenge the dominance of traditional exchanges.
- **Tokenization of Assets:** We're not just talking cryptocurrencies anymore. Real-world assets like real estate, art, and even private company shares are being tokenized on the blockchain, opening up new markets and investment opportunities.
- **Smart Contracts:** These self-executing contracts automatically enforce the terms of a trade, reducing the need for intermediaries and increasing efficiency.

3. **Quantum Computing: The Speed of Light (Almost)**
- **Exponential Processing Power:** While still in its early stages, quantum computing has the potential to revolutionize market microstructure by solving complex calculations at unprecedented speeds. This could give traders a massive edge in analyzing data, optimizing portfolios, and executing trades.
- **Risk Modeling and Optimization:** Quantum algorithms could create incredibly sophisticated risk models and optimization strategies, leading to more efficient portfolio management and risk mitigation.

4. **Big Data and Alternative Data: The Information Goldmine**
- **Unstructured Data Unleashed:** It's not just about price and volume anymore. Traders are tapping into a wealth of alternative data, including satellite imagery, social media sentiment, credit card transactions, and even shipping data, to gain unique insights into market trends and company performance.
- **Data Analytics Advancements:** Machine learning algorithms are becoming adept at extracting valuable signals from this unstructured data, giving traders a potential edge.

5. **Internet of Things (IoT): The Sensor Network**
- **Real-Time Market Intelligence:** Imagine sensors embedded in shipping containers, retail stores, or manufacturing plants, transmitting real-time data about supply chains, inventory levels, and consumer behavior. This data could provide valuable insights into market trends and demand patterns.

The Challenges Ahead:

- **Regulatory Landscape:** These emerging technologies raise new regulatory challenges, requiring policymakers to adapt existing rules or create new ones to ensure fair and orderly markets.
- **Data Privacy and Security:** The increasing reliance on data raises concerns about privacy, security breaches, and potential misuse of information.
- **Unequal Access:** Not all market participants have equal access to cutting-edge technology, potentially creating an uneven playing field.

Evolution of Trading Practices

1. The Rise of Algorithmic and High-Frequency Trading (HFT):

- **From Human to Machine:** Trading floors once buzzed with human voices and hand signals. Now, powerful algorithms dominate, executing trades at speeds unimaginable to human traders.
- **Benefits:** Algorithmic trading has brought increased liquidity, tighter spreads, and greater efficiency to markets.
- **Challenges:** The speed and complexity of these systems raise concerns about market stability, fairness, and the potential for unintended consequences.

2. The Democratization of Trading:

- **Empowering Retail Investors:** Online brokerage platforms and commission-free trading apps have made it easier than ever for individual investors to participate in markets.
- **Social Trading:** Platforms like eToro and Robinhood allow users to follow and copy the trades of successful investors, opening up new avenues for learning and engagement.
- **Challenges:** The influx of retail traders has introduced new volatility and, at times, irrational exuberance to markets.

3. The Fragmentation of Markets:

- **Multiple Trading Venues:** Trading activity is no longer confined to traditional exchanges. Alternative trading systems (ATS), dark pools, and even decentralized exchanges (DEXs) now offer diverse options for executing trades.
- **Complex Order Routing:** Brokers utilize sophisticated algorithms to route orders to the best possible venue, optimizing execution costs and prices.
- **Challenges:** Fragmentation can make it harder to track prices and understand overall market dynamics. It can also lead to concerns about fairness and transparency.

4. The Rise of Sustainable and Impact Investing:

- **Ethical Considerations:** Investors are increasingly incorporating environmental, social, and governance (ESG) factors into their investment decisions.
- **Impact on Trading:** This trend is influencing the types of securities being traded and the strategies employed by investors. We can expect to see more demand for sustainable investments and greater scrutiny of companies' ESG practices.

5. The Growing Importance of Data and Analytics:

- **Data-Driven Decision Making:** Traders and investors are increasingly relying on data and analytics to gain insights into market trends, identify opportunities, and manage risk.
- **Alternative Data:** Unconventional data sources like satellite imagery, social media sentiment, and credit card transactions are being mined for valuable signals.
- **Challenges:** The sheer volume and complexity of data require sophisticated tools and expertise to analyze effectively.

6. The Shift Towards Passive Investing:

- **Index Funds and ETFs:** The popularity of passive investing, through vehicles like index funds and exchange-traded funds (ETFs), continues to grow. This is driven by the belief that it's difficult to consistently beat the market and the desire for lower fees.
- **Impact on Active Management:** This trend is putting pressure on active fund managers to justify their higher fees and demonstrate consistent outperformance.

7. The Integration of Artificial Intelligence (AI):

- **Predictive Analytics:** AI algorithms are being used to forecast market trends, optimize trading strategies, and manage risk more effectively.
- **Sentiment Analysis:** AI can analyze vast amounts of textual data to gauge market sentiment and predict its impact on prices.
- **Challenges:** The "black box" nature of some AI algorithms raises concerns about transparency and accountability.

Future Regulatory and Market Structure Changes

The winds of change are blowing, and they could bring both opportunities and challenges.

Regulatory Trends:

1. **Increased Scrutiny of High-Frequency Trading (HFT):**
   - **Concerns:** Regulators are increasingly concerned about the impact of HFT on market fairness, stability, and the potential for manipulation.
   - **Potential Actions:**
     - **Tighter Restrictions:** We may see stricter rules on order-to-trade ratios, cancellation rates, and other HFT practices.
     - **Speed Bumps:** Regulators might introduce artificial delays or randomizations in order processing to level the playing field between HFT firms and other market participants.
     - **Enhanced Surveillance:** Expect greater monitoring and surveillance of HFT activity to detect and deter manipulative practices.

2. **Addressing Market Fragmentation:**
   - **Concerns:** The proliferation of trading venues has fragmented liquidity, making it harder to find the best prices and understand market dynamics.
   - **Potential Actions:**
     - **Consolidated Tape:** A centralized feed of trade data from all venues could improve transparency and price discovery.

- **Minimum Pricing Increments:** Standardizing tick sizes across venues could reduce complexity and make it easier to compare prices.
- **Order Routing Rules:** Tighter rules on order routing could prevent brokers from favoring certain venues or engaging in practices that harm market quality.

3. **Regulation of Crypto Markets:**
- **Concerns:** The rapid growth of crypto markets has raised concerns about investor protection, market manipulation, and systemic risk.
- **Potential Actions:**
  - **Licensing and Registration:** Cryptocurrency exchanges and other market participants may be required to obtain licenses and adhere to stricter regulatory requirements.
  - **Custody Rules:** Safeguarding of customer assets and clear segregation of funds may become mandatory.
  - **Market Surveillance:** Increased monitoring of trading activity to detect and prevent market manipulation.

4. **Enhanced Investor Protection:**
- **Concerns:** The rise of complex financial products and high-speed trading has created new risks for investors.
- **Potential Actions:**
  - **Suitability Requirements:** Stricter rules to ensure that financial products are suitable for the investors they are sold to.
  - **Disclosure Requirements:** Enhanced disclosure of fees, risks, and conflicts of interest to empower investors to make informed decisions.
  - **Best Execution:** Stricter enforcement of best execution rules to ensure that brokers get the best possible prices for their clients.

Market Structure Changes:

1. **The Rise of Decentralized Finance (DeFi):**
- **Decentralized Exchanges (DEXs):** These peer-to-peer trading platforms could challenge the dominance of traditional exchanges, offering greater transparency and potentially lower costs.
- **Automated Market Makers (AMMs):** These algorithms provide liquidity in DeFi markets, potentially replacing traditional market makers.

2. **Evolution of Market Data:**
- **Consolidated Tape:** A single, unified view of market data across all venues could improve transparency and price discovery.
- **Real-Time Data:** Faster and more granular data feeds could enable more sophisticated trading strategies and risk management.

3. **The Role of Artificial Intelligence (AI):**
   - **AI-Powered Trading:** AI will play an increasingly important role in trading, from developing complex strategies to executing orders with lightning speed.
   - **AI-Driven Market Surveillance:** Regulators will leverage AI to detect market manipulation and other illicit activities.

4. **Sustainable Finance:**
   - **ESG Considerations:** Environmental, social, and governance (ESG) factors will become increasingly important in investment decisions, potentially influencing market structure and trading practices.

Technology, regulation, and investor preferences are all evolving rapidly, and the markets of tomorrow are likely to look very different from those of today. By staying informed and adaptable, you can navigate this changing landscape and seize the opportunities that emerge.

APPENDIX

Terms and Definitions

Market Microstructure: The study of the processes and mechanisms through which securities are traded, including the ways in which prices are determined.

Order Book: A record of the buy and sell orders for a specific security organized by price level.

Bid Price: The highest price a buyer is willing to pay for a security.

Ask Price: The lowest price a seller is willing to accept for a security.

Bid-Ask Spread: The difference between the bid price and the ask price.

Limit Order: An order to buy or sell a security at a specific price or better.

Market Order: An order to buy or sell a security immediately at the best available current price.

Liquidity: The ease with which a security can be bought or sold without affecting its price.

Depth: The number of shares that can be traded at the best bid and ask prices without affecting the price.

Market Maker: A firm or individual that provides liquidity by buying and selling securities at publicly quoted prices.

High-Frequency Trading (HFT): A type of trading that uses powerful computers and algorithms to execute large numbers of orders at extremely high speeds.

Dark Pool: A private financial forum or exchange for trading securities, not accessible by the public.

Arbitrage: The simultaneous purchase and sale of the same asset in different markets to profit from price discrepancies.

Clearing House: An intermediary between buyers and sellers of financial instruments that ensures the integrity and efficiency of transactions.

Settlement: The process by which a trade is completed, involving the transfer of securities and funds between the buyer and seller.

Tick Size: The minimum price movement of a trading instrument.

Price Discovery: The process through which the price of an asset is determined by the interactions of buyers and sellers.

Order Flow: The buying and selling activity of investors in the market.

Execution: The completion of a buy or sell order.

Slippage: The difference between the expected price of a trade and the actual price at which it is executed.

Front Running: The unethical practice of a broker executing orders on a security for its own account while taking advantage of advance knowledge of pending orders from its customers.

Latency: The delay between the initiation of a market order and its execution.

Market Impact: The effect that a trade has on the price of the security being traded.

Broker: An individual or firm that acts as an intermediary between buyers and sellers of securities.

Agency Trade: A trade executed by a broker on behalf of a client.

Principal Trade: A trade executed by a broker-dealer who buys or sells for their own account.

Stop Order: An order to buy or sell a security once the price reaches a specified level.

Fill or Kill Order (FOK): An order that must be executed immediately and completely or not at all.

All or None Order (AON): An order that must be executed in its entirety or not at all.

Immediate or Cancel Order (IOC): An order to buy or sell that must be executed immediately. Any portion not executed is canceled.

Day Order: An order that is good for the trading day and will expire at the end of the day if not executed.

Good Till Canceled (GTC): An order that remains active until it is executed or canceled by the trader.

Opening Order: An order to be executed at the opening of the market.

Closing Order: An order to be executed at the close of the market.

Pegged Order: An order whose price is pegged to a reference price, such as the best bid or offer.

Stop-Limit Order: A stop order that becomes a limit order once the stop price is reached.

Iceberg Order: A large order that is divided into smaller visible orders to avoid moving the market price.

Odd Lot: A quantity of securities that is less than the standard unit of trading.

Round Lot: The standard trading unit, typically 100 shares for stocks.

Block Trade: A large trade, typically involving 10,000 shares or more.

Algorithmic Trading: The use of computer algorithms to execute trades based on predefined criteria.

Smart Order Routing (SOR): Technology that routes orders to various market centers to achieve the best execution.

Quote: The current bid and ask prices for a security.

Spread Betting: A speculative strategy where the participant bets on the price movement of a security.

Exchange-Traded Fund (ETF): A type of investment fund traded on stock exchanges, much like stocks.

Market Capitalization: The total market value of a company's outstanding shares of stock.

Initial Public Offering (IPO): The first sale of a company's stock to the public.

Secondary Market: The market where previously issued securities are traded.

Primary Market: The market where new securities are issued and sold for the first time.

Dealer: An individual or firm that buys and sells securities for their own account.

Liquidity Provider: A market participant that makes a two-sided market, providing both buy and sell quotes.

Circuit Breaker: Measures used to temporarily halt trading on an exchange to curb panic-selling.

Crossing Network: A type of alternative trading system where buy and sell orders are matched anonymously.

Auction Market: A market where buyers and sellers enter competitive bids simultaneously.

Electronic Communication Network (ECN): An automated system that matches buy and sell orders for securities.

Price Limit: The maximum range that a security's price is allowed to increase or decrease in a single trading session.

Margin: The collateral that an investor must deposit to borrow funds for trading securities.

Short Selling: The sale of a security that the seller does not own, with the intention of buying it back at a lower price.

Bear Market: A market characterized by falling prices.

Bull Market: A market characterized by rising prices.

Stop-Loss Order: An order placed to sell a security when it reaches a certain price to limit losses.

Limit-Up Limit-Down (LULD): Mechanisms to prevent trades in individual securities from occurring outside of specified price bands.

Spoofing: The illegal practice of placing orders with the intent to cancel them before execution to manipulate prices.

Layering: A form of market manipulation involving the placement of multiple orders on one side of the market to create a false impression of demand or supply.

Tick: The minimum upward or downward movement in the price of a security.

Volatility: A statistical measure of the dispersion of returns for a given security or market index.

Liquidity Risk: The risk that an entity will not be able to meet its short-term financial obligations due to an inability to liquidate assets.

Market Depth: The market's ability to sustain relatively large market orders without impacting the price of the security.

Quote Stuffing: The practice of quickly entering and then withdrawing large quantities of orders to create confusion and slow down competitors.

Rebate: A fee paid by an exchange to brokers or traders who provide liquidity.

Flash Crash: A very rapid, deep, and volatile fall in security prices occurring within an extremely short time period.

Volume Weighted Average Price (VWAP): A trading benchmark calculated by taking the average price a security has traded at throughout the day, based on both volume and price.

Index Arbitrage: A trading strategy that attempts to profit from differences between the price of a stock index and its constituent stocks.

Order Flow Analysis: The examination of the order flow in the market to predict future price movements.

Latency Arbitrage: Exploiting price differences in markets due to delays in information transmission.

Market Depth Chart: A graphical representation of the bid and ask prices for a security, along with the volume of orders at each price level.

Execution Venue: The marketplace where a trade is executed, such as a stock exchange or alternative trading system.

Regulation NMS: A set of rules passed by the SEC in 2005 to modernize and strengthen the National Market System for equity securities.

Maker-Taker Model: A pricing model used by exchanges where liquidity providers (makers) receive rebates and liquidity takers (takers) are charged fees.

Short Interest: The total number of shares of a particular stock that have been sold short but have not yet been covered or closed out.

Payment for Order Flow: The compensation and benefit a brokerage firm receives for directing orders to different parties for trade execution.

Real-Time Market Data: Information about current prices and trades that is available immediately after the transactions occur.

Trade Reporting Facility (TRF): A facility for reporting transactions that occur off-exchange.

Alternative Trading System (ATS): A trading venue that is not regulated as an exchange but is a venue for matching the buy and sell orders of its subscribers.

Portfolio Trading: The trading of a group of securities, usually managed together within a portfolio, rather than individual securities.

Market Depth Information: Data showing the amount of pending buy and sell orders at different price levels for a particular asset.

Synthetic Order Book: A virtual order book created by combining data from multiple sources to provide a comprehensive view of market liquidity.

Book Skew: Book skew refers to the imbalance in the order book, where there is a significant disparity between the number of buy orders and sell orders at various price levels, potentially indicating future price movements.

FAQs

What is market microstructure?

Market microstructure is the study of the processes and mechanisms through which securities are traded. It encompasses the rules, systems, and practices that determine how trades are executed, how prices are formed, and how market participants interact. This field examines the functioning of financial markets at a granular level, focusing on the behavior of traders, the structure of order books, and the impact of regulations.

How does market microstructure impact trading efficiency?

Market microstructure significantly impacts trading efficiency by influencing the speed and cost of trade execution. Efficient market structures facilitate quicker and cheaper trades, reducing transaction costs and improving liquidity. Conversely, inefficient structures can lead to higher costs, slower execution times, and reduced market liquidity. Elements such as order types, trading platforms, and regulatory frameworks all are important in determining overall trading efficiency.

What are the key components of market microstructure?

Key components of market microstructure include:

- **Order Types:** Various orders like market orders, limit orders, stop orders, etc.
- **Order Book:** The electronic list of buy and sell orders for a specific security.
- **Market Participants:** Traders, brokers, market makers, and high-frequency traders.
- **Trading Venues:** Stock exchanges, electronic communication networks (ECNs), and dark pools.
- **Regulations:** Rules and guidelines that govern market operations and trading practices.

- **Price Discovery:** The process through which market prices are determined through interactions between buyers and sellers.
- **Liquidity:** The ease with which assets can be bought or sold in the market without affecting their price.

How do bid and ask prices affect market liquidity?

Bid and ask prices are critical in determining market liquidity. The bid price represents the highest price a buyer is willing to pay, while the ask price is the lowest price a seller is willing to accept. The difference between these prices, known as the bid-ask spread, indicates the liquidity of the market. A narrow spread suggests high liquidity, meaning assets can be quickly bought or sold with minimal price impact. A wider spread indicates lower liquidity, as there is less agreement between buyers and sellers on the price.

What is the role of market makers in market microstructure?

Market makers are vital in market microstructure by providing liquidity and ensuring smoother trading operations. They do this by continuously quoting buy and sell prices for securities, thus enabling other market participants to execute trades efficiently. Market makers profit from the bid-ask spread but also take on the risk of holding inventory. Their presence helps reduce price volatility and enhances market stability by ensuring that there are always counterparties available for trades.

How do high-frequency traders influence market microstructure?

High-frequency traders (HFTs) influence market microstructure through their use of advanced algorithms and high-speed trading strategies. They provide liquidity by placing a large number of orders at different price levels and executing trades in milliseconds. HFTs can improve market efficiency by narrowing bid-ask spreads and enhancing price discovery. However, their activities can also increase market volatility and pose risks of market manipulation, such as quote stuffing or latency arbitrage.

What are dark pools, and how do they function within market microstructure?

Dark pools are private trading venues where buy and sell orders are not displayed publicly before execution. They allow large institutional investors to execute sizable trades without revealing their intentions to the broader market, thereby minimizing market impact and reducing the risk of price slippage. Within market microstructure, dark pools contribute to overall liquidity but also raise concerns about market transparency and fairness, as they can obscure true market depth and price discovery.

How does order flow contribute to price discovery?

Order flow, the aggregate of all buy and sell orders in the market, is a fundamental element in price discovery. It reflects the supply and demand dynamics for a security. When buy orders outweigh sell orders, prices tend to rise, and vice versa. Analyzing order flow helps traders and market participants gauge market sentiment and predict future price movements. Continuous interaction of order flow leads to the formation of fair market prices over time.

What is the significance of the bid-ask spread in market microstructure?

The bid-ask spread is a key indicator of market liquidity and transaction costs. A narrow bid-ask spread signifies a liquid market where assets can be traded quickly with minimal price impact, benefiting traders through lower transaction costs. Conversely, a wide bid-ask spread indicates a less liquid market, higher transaction costs, and greater uncertainty about the true market value of an asset. The bid-ask spread also reflects the risk perception and inventory costs of market makers.

How do different order types (e.g., limit orders, market orders) affect trading?

Different order types impact trading dynamics in various ways:

- **Market Orders:** These are executed immediately at the best available current price, ensuring quick execution but with potential price slippage in volatile markets.
- **Limit Orders:** These specify the maximum or minimum price at which a trader is willing to buy or sell. They provide price control but may not be executed if the market does not reach the specified price.
- **Stop Orders:** These trigger a market order once a specified price is reached, helping traders limit losses or lock in profits.
- **Fill or Kill Orders (FOK):** These must be executed immediately in their entirety or not at all, ensuring no partial fills but risking non-execution.

Each order type affects liquidity, price discovery, and trading strategies differently, contributing to the overall complexity of market microstructure.

What are the implications of market depth for traders and investors?

Market depth refers to the market's ability to absorb large orders without significantly impacting the price of a security. Deep markets with substantial buy and sell orders at various price levels indicate high liquidity, allowing traders and investors to execute large trades with minimal price movement. Shallow markets, on the other hand, suggest lower liquidity and greater price volatility. Understanding market depth helps traders anticipate the potential price impact of their orders and make informed trading decisions.

How do trading venues like ECNs and dark pools differ in market microstructure?

Electronic Communication Networks (ECNs) and dark pools are alternative trading venues with distinct roles in market microstructure:

- **ECNs:** These are automated systems that match buy and sell orders from multiple participants, often offering lower transaction costs and faster execution. ECNs display orders publicly, contributing to market transparency and efficient price discovery.
- **Dark Pools:** These private trading venues do not display orders publicly before execution. They allow large trades to be executed anonymously, reducing market impact and price slippage. However, dark pools can obscure market depth and raise concerns about market fairness and transparency.

What role does latency play in high-frequency trading?

Latency, the delay between the initiation and execution of a trade, is a critical factor in high-frequency trading (HFT). HFT strategies rely on extremely low latency to capitalize on minute price differences across markets. Reducing latency can enhance the speed and efficiency of trade execution, providing HFT firms with a competitive advantage. However, latency can also create risks, such as the potential for trades to be executed based on outdated information, leading to increased market volatility and potential systemic risks.

How does slippage impact trade execution?

Slippage occurs when there is a difference between the expected price of a trade and the actual execution price. It is particularly common in fast-moving or illiquid markets. Slippage can result in higher trading costs and reduced profitability for traders. It affects market participants by introducing uncertainty and risk into the trading process. Effective strategies to minimize slippage include using limit orders, trading during times of high liquidity, and avoiding large orders that may significantly impact prices.

What are the effects of front running on market fairness?

Front running is an unethical practice where a broker executes orders on a security for its own account while taking advantage of advance knowledge of pending orders from its customers. This practice undermines market fairness by giving the broker an unfair advantage, leading to potential losses for clients and erosion of trust in the market. Front running can distort market prices, reduce market efficiency, and result in regulatory scrutiny and penalties for the offending parties.

How do regulatory measures like circuit breakers influence market microstructure?

Circuit breakers are regulatory measures designed to temporarily halt trading on an exchange to curb panic-selling and excessive volatility. They are triggered when a security or market index experiences a significant price decline within a short period. Circuit breakers provide a cooling-off period for market participants to assess information and make rational decisions, thereby stabilizing the market. While they help prevent extreme market movements, they can also interrupt normal trading activities and affect market liquidity.

What is the importance of clearing houses in trade settlement?

Clearing houses are necessary in trade settlement by acting as intermediaries between buyers and sellers. They ensure the integrity and efficiency of transactions by confirming trade details, netting obligations, and facilitating the transfer of securities and funds. Clearing houses mitigate counterparty risk by guaranteeing the performance of each trade, thereby enhancing market stability and confidence. They also streamline the settlement process, reducing the time and complexity involved in trade finalization.

How does the maker-taker model affect trading behavior?

The maker-taker model is a pricing structure used by exchanges where liquidity providers (makers) receive rebates for adding liquidity, while liquidity takers (takers) are charged fees for removing liquidity. This model incentivizes market participants to provide liquidity by placing limit orders, thereby enhancing market depth and stability. However, it can also lead to complex fee structures and potential conflicts of interest, as traders and brokers may prioritize venues based on rebates rather than best execution for clients.

What are the risks associated with spoofing and layering in the market?

Spoofing and layering are forms of market manipulation where traders place large orders with the intent to cancel them before execution, creating a false impression of demand or supply. These practices can distort market prices, mislead other market participants, and undermine market integrity. Spoofing and layering increase volatility and can lead to significant financial losses for traders who rely on accurate market signals. Regulatory authorities impose strict penalties to deter such manipulative behaviors and maintain market fairness.

How do market microstructure changes influence overall market stability?

Changes in market microstructure, such as new trading technologies, regulatory reforms, and evolving trading strategies, can significantly impact overall market stability. Enhancements in market infrastructure can improve efficiency, liquidity, and price discovery, contributing to a more stable and robust market environment. Conversely, rapid changes or inadequate regulations can introduce new risks, increase volatility, and create opportunities for market manipulation. Continuous monitoring and adaptation of market microstructure are essential to maintaining a balanced and resilient financial system.

AFTERWORD

Throughout this book, we've looked into the mechanisms that govern the behavior of financial markets, exploring the interplay between various participants, processes, and technologies.

One of the key takeaways from our exploration is the impact that market microstructure has on the overall functioning and efficiency of financial markets. We've learned that the structure of markets, the rules that govern trading, and the roles played by intermediaries like market makers and high-frequency traders, all have a significant influence on price formation, liquidity, and market stability.

We gained a deeper understanding of the importance of market liquidity and the factors that contribute to it. We explored the dynamics of order flow and order book imbalances, and how these can drive price movements. Additionally, we looked into the concept of market efficiency and the limitations of the Efficient Market Hypothesis, recognizing that market anomalies and patterns can sometimes persist due to various frictions and constraints.

Our journey also shed light on the critical role played by market makers in providing liquidity and facilitating smooth trading. We examined the strategies they employ, the risks they face, and the regulatory frameworks that govern their activities. Moreover, we explored the world of trading strategies, from traditional arbitrage techniques to cutting-edge algorithmic and high-frequency trading approaches, recognizing the constant evolution and innovation in this field.

Importantly, we acknowledged the behavioral aspects of trading, examining the psychological biases and emotional factors that can influence decision-making in the markets. Understanding these dynamics is important for developing a well-rounded perspective on market microstructure and making informed investment decisions.

Throughout, we looked at impact of technology on market microstructure. From the rise of high-frequency trading to the advent of cryptocurrencies and decentralized finance, we observed how technological advancements are continuously reshaping the trading landscape, introducing new opportunities and challenges alike.

As we looked ahead to the future, we recognize that the field of market microstructure is evolving, with emerging technologies, regulatory changes, and shifts in market structure set to shape its trajectory. The potential impact of artificial intelligence, machine learning, and the evolving regulatory landscape will influence the way financial markets operate in the years to come.

Printed in Great Britain
by Amazon